SOCCER
AND
SPEEDBALL
FOR WOMEN

PHYSICAL EDUCATION ACTIVITIES SERIES

Consulting Editor:
AILEENE LOCKHART
University of Southern California
Los Angeles, California

Evaluation Materials Editor:
JANE A. MOTT
Smith College
Northampton, Massachusetts

SOCCER
AND
SPEEDBALL
FOR WOMEN

JANE A. MOTT
Smith College

Technique Illustrations by WILLO CAREY

WM. C. BROWN COMPANY PUBLISHERS
Dubuque, Iowa

Contents

Preface

Soccer and speedball are closely related field sports which share many techniques, rules, tactics, and much basic team strategy. For this reason it has been possible to present in one relatively small volume a considerable amount of information about both sports for the novice and the more experienced player.

This book has been designed primarily as a text for the college student enrolled in a physical education activity course, although the content is appropriate for all players and teachers of soccer and speedball. Step by step nontechnical descriptions of techniques supplemented by numerous illustrations make it possible to work independently to perfect skills. The novice should concentrate particularly on the techniques in chapter 2, "Skills Essential for Everyone," while the player with some experience will wish to acquire the skills in chapter 3, "Better Players Master These Techniques."

Independent practice is stressed in chapter 5. Here the reader will find information on fitness and conditioning for soccer and speedball as well as drills for one, two, or three or more players. Some of the skills can be scored for self-testing purposes. Evaluation questions interspersed throughout the book also enable the student to check her own progress informally. Both the drills and the evaluation questions are representative of the kinds of learnings that should be taking place. The serious student will devise similar questions and other drills as further self-checks.

A condensation of the rules of the games, terms and definitions, historical and contemporary perspectives, and a list of supplementary references complete the topics covered in the book.

An overlap system of organization has been utilized in the contents in order to emphasize the commonalities of the sports and to avoid repetitious descriptions and the inconvenience of page hopping. Wherever information applies both to soccer and speedball it appears as a separate section of a chapter. This overlapping content is then supplemented by sections directed specifically to soccer and to speedball.

What Soccer and Speedball are Like

1

Soccer

Universal in its attraction, soccer is the most popular of all team sports, far outranking American football, basketball, and baseball. The men's game is played in approximately 130 nations, virtually every country in the world. Furthermore, the fervor of the spectators equals that of the participants. More than 800 million people were estimated to have witnessed the televised finals of the 1970 World Cup match. Watching in person were 108,000 people and 112,000 others had to be turned away at the gate. England alone is reported to have 16,000 *referees* and Russia has 3.8 million players. A soccer stadium in Brazil seats 200,000 spectators. It is thought that more than one billion people follow international play. Victory calls for carnivals and frenzied celebration; defeat brings national despair. Soccer is plainly a challenging game to play, an exciting game to watch.

The sport masquerades under different names: while it is "soccer" in the United States, it is most commonly called "football" in the rest of the world. Conjecture has it that the name may have derived from "assoc." the abbreviation of "association football" as the game is titled by the British, or from the fact that players often wear knee socks, or from the rough play ("socker") which characterized the contests of a hundred or more years ago.

Soccer for both men and women is primarily a running and kicking field sport, the object being to score points by causing the ball to pass through the opposing team's goal. Eleven players comprise a team. The center forward, left and right inners, and the left and right wings make up the forward line, which stretches across the width of the field. Behind the forwards are the left, center, and right halfbacks, followed by the left and right fullbacks. Finally comes the goalkeeper, whose action is generally confined to the vincinity of the goal, which is formed by posts 18 feet apart joined by a crossbar 8 feet high. The official playing field dimensions are 40-60 yards by 80-100 yards, and the playing surface is usually turf.

The game begins with each team in its own half of the field; that is, the end with the goal the team is defending (fig. 1). A forward kicks the ball from the center of the field into her opponents' territory and thereafter the teams skirmish to advance the ball through the mouth of the opponents' goal and to thwart the other team in its efforts to do the same. Throwing

1

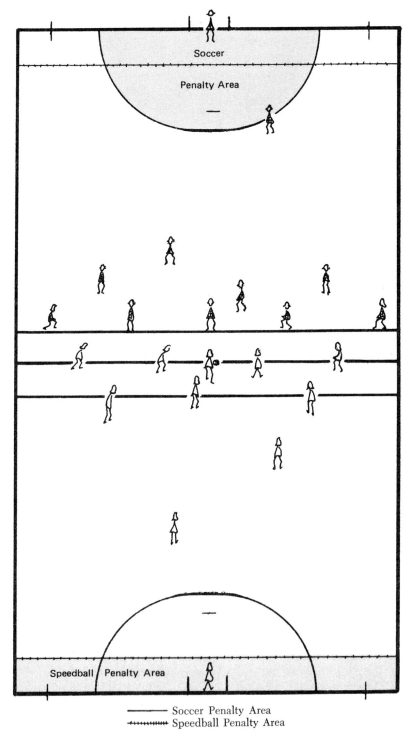

Soccer

Penalty Area

Speedball | Penalty Area

——————— Soccer Penalty Area
+++++++++++++ Speedball Penalty Area

Figure 1—The Kick-off in Soccer or Speedball

the ball is legal only for the goalkeeper within the penalty area or for a player who is putting an out-of-bounds ball back into play across the side-line. The game is divided into four 8-minute quarters with a 10-minute rest between halves and a 2-minute interval after the first and third quarters.

Such a mundane description of soccer fails, however, to convey the essence of the sport. Soccer is a game of continuous, free-flowing action, a fast-paced shifting of patterns in response to each move of the ball. For the most part, play is spontaneous and open, permitting any team member to take the initiative in redirecting the immediate course of events. Rules are simple, set plays are few, but the speed of a hard-kicked ball can reach 95 miles per hour, and this demands alert reactions, a high level of stamina, and exceptional control. Above all, soccer is a team endeavor. Skillful play is a masterpiece of cooperation, a synchronization of the purposes, actions, and attitudes of eleven individuals. Each must be appropriately aggressive in his own role, supportive in relation to the play of his teammates.

Oddly enough, even though men's soccer is much more highly acclaimed in countries outside the United States, it is *only* in the United States that there are feminine participants in the sport. Here, girls and women enjoy soccer mainly in school and college settings. The rudiments of team play are often introduced during the junior high school years. Finesse in indi-vidual technique and the smooth harmony of a group of players working as a unit develop gradually with experience in physical education classes in secondary schools and colleges. Very little opportunity has been afforded thus far for women to participate in soccer in the community or on a club basis, as is the case in field hockey and lacrosse, but this may well come in time, particularly if other countries also adapt the men's rules for women's play. In the meantime, soccer stands on its own merits as a "here and now" school opportunity, excellent as a physical conditioner, mentally challeng-ing, and above all, great fun.

Speedball

Speedball is a surprisingly compatible mix of soccer, basketball, and a few elements of football. The ingredients combine to form a unique and exciting sport calling for versatility on the part of the players. Essentially, speedball is a field sport involving running, kicking, and throwing in which two teams compete for score by trying to advance the ball across the oppo-nents' goal line in any of several designated ways. A general idea of the game can be had by visualizing the setting as a soccer field with one dif-ference in field markings: the quarter circles outlining the soccer penalty area are erased; instead, the penalty area is rectangular, lying between the goal line and a line parallel to it but 5 yards within the field. The goal is the same as for soccer except that the posts must be 20 feet high. The eleven players on a team are named and positioned as they are for soccer. The kickoff also is the same as for soccer (see fig. 1, p. 2). After the action begins, it is governed in general by soccer rules while the ball is on the ground and by basketball rules when the ball is designated as "aerial."

The ball may be propelled by any of the means used in soccer. Also, provided the ball has been lofted directly from a kick, it becomes an aerial ball and may be caught with the hands or be thrown. Once an aerial ball touches the ground, it reverts to ground ball status and cannot be handled until it is lifted again by playing it with the feet.

Points are earned by kicking or volleying a ground ball between the goal posts under the crossbar, by dropkicking over the crossbar, or by a throw from the field of play which is caught by a teammate behind the opponents' goal line.

Despite the seeming complexities of such a truly hybrid sport, speedball is as fast moving as the name implies. Many novices are already familiar with soccer and basketball and so need learn only a few new rules and several novel techniques. The great variety of legal means of playing the ball gives even the neophyte sufficient choice so that she can be reasonably effective with skills she already possesses. Fouls are relatively infrequent owing to the freedom of movement in the large playing area, and scoring is easier than in soccer or field hockey.

Although the women's game of speedball was adapted from the rules for men, the sport has gained more popularity with feminine players than with masculine and is enjoyed in many schools and colleges during the fall season. The individual initiative, vigorous movement, and challenging interaction of soccer team play are provided in full measure by speedball but there is less position specialization than in soccer. Rather, each player takes a more equal part in all aspects of the game.

Equipment

Playing equipment for soccer and speedball is simple. The ball, a lined field, and goal posts are the basics. Essential personal attire includes shorts, kilt, or tunic, a blouse, socks, and low-cut or high sneakers. Leather shoes or shoes with a rubber or leather disc over the inner ankle bone, extra toe tips, and rubber cleats may be worn and are advised for intermediate and advanced players. The rules bar the wearing of metal plates or projecting heavy soles. Novices learn the "feel" of the ball best in ordinary sneakers without extra toe protection or cleats. Whatever the shoe, the laces should be tied at the side of the shoe tongue so that the ball and the knot will not meet on instep kicks.

Shin guards are not an absolute requirement but are a great protection and give the novice confidence in meeting the ball with the shin. Field hockey shin guards will do, but may interfere with kicks using the side of the foot. The relatively small shin guards worn under knee socks and held in place by them are much preferred by most players.

The goalkeeper requires no special equipment but may wish to wear a warmup suit or slacks for greater comfort in fielding hard-kicked shots at the goal. The color of the goalkeeper's apparel should distinguish her from other players so that the umpire can easily identify the player who has goalkeeper privileges in soccer.

Pinnies are an important aid to the players and to the officials when the clothing of the two teams is not markedly different. If necessary, only one team need wear pinnies, but preferably both teams are so attired in different colors and with the initials of each position in large letters across the back.

Safety

Soccer and speedball are noncontact sports under the rules for women's play, and the incidence of injuries is relatively low. Nevertheless, an occasional mishap occurs and when it does it is most apt to be a bruise, abrasion, pulled muscle, or a joint injury. The risks can be minimized if simple precautions are taken in practice and competition.

Preliminaries to Play

1. Inspect the field for holes, foreign objects, uneven or slippery surface, condition of goal posts, and obstacles near boundaries.
2. Wear shin guards and appropriate clothing which cannot interfere with running and playing the ball, or hurt another player.
3. Remove jewelry and secure hair if it is long.
4. Wear glasses guards if your glasses do not have safety lenses. As goalkeeper, wear guards regardless of the type of lenses.
5. Warm up well before vigorous practice or play.

During Play

1. Play your position, only one teammate on the ball.
2. Aim before you kick. Never kick hard directly at a player from short range.
3. Head only those balls above chest level and jump to meet the ball with the front or side of the head only.
4. Don't let your weight go onto the ball when trapping.
5. Aim carefully at the ball when tackling.

2 Skills Essential for Everyone

All techniques involving actual contact with the ball serve one of two main purposes or a combination of both: *propulsion* and *control*.

Propelling the Ball

Propelling the ball by kicking it is a fundamental skill in both soccer and speedball, and various means of effectively advancing the ball by utilizing the instep, inside, outside, heel, and even sole of the foot have been developed. In addition, the ball may be blocked; that is, it may be allowed to rebound from any part of the body or legs, or from the arms under certain circumstances. Use of the hands and arms to block is always legal for aerial balls in speedball, but for ground balls, or for any ball in soccer, the hands and arms must be held entirely in contact with the body. When the head is used to block the ball, the technique is called "heading." Finally, the ball may be propelled in designated circumstances by throwing it with one or two hands.

Basics of All Propulsive Actions

1. Preliminary to contact with the ball, widen the base and lower the center of gravity for good balance (stride stance and flexed knees).
2. Keep eyes on the ball until contact with it.
3. Decide on the point of aim.
4. Use the arms and legs in opposition for good balance.
5. Take a full relaxed backswing and a good follow-through whenever possible.

Basics of Kicking

1. Align the body so that the proper surface of the foot will be presented to the ball.
2. Remember that trajectory depends on the point of contact on the ball. A point below center lofts the ball, at center results in a straight trajectory until gravity takes over, and above center directs the ball downward. If the foot meets the ball at the left of center, the kick will cause spin and a trajectory which curves to the right. The opposite effect is brought about by a contact to the right of center.

3. If a long, low kick is intended, make sure body weight is moving forward into the kick and is as nearly over the ball as possible at the moment of impact.
4. Note that accuracy is best when the ball is met with a large surface, when it is stationary or nearly so as it is kicked, and when it is returned in the direction from which it came.

Types of Kicks

INSTEP KICK (fig. 2). There are many times during a soccer or speedball game when a player will want to send the ball forcefully. In shooting for goal or taking a free kick, for example, the speed with which the ball travels

Figure 2—The Instep Kick

may determine whether the play is successful or is intercepted. In clearing the ball from in front of the goal or in passing to a teammate down the field, good distance may be essential to the kicker's purpose. In these and other situations the instep kick is highly useful. Fortunately, it is also the most natural and easy-to-learn method of propelling the ball with the foot. If one stands on one foot and swings the other leg well back and then forward this gives the general idea of the kicking motion. The driving force comes from a forward shift of body weight to the supporting foot, the momentum of the kicking leg, and the properly timed explosive extension of the knee joint. There is no need to worry about arm motion in this or any other kick as the balancing movements are instinctive in reaction to the kicking pattern.

1. With the ball stationary and your eyes fixed on it throughout, step forward to place the non-kicking foot even with the ball and about 4-6 inches to the side.
2. Keep this knee slightly bent and the toes pointed toward the target while lifting the kicking leg backward so that it can start its forward swing from a position with the hip extended and the knee flexed.
3. While holding the kicking ankle firm and toes pointed, swing the leg directly forward to meet the ball with your shoe lace contacting its

horizontal axis. The knee of the kicking foot is over the ball upon impact and slightly flexed.

4. Take a follow-through that brings the kicking leg to full extension forward to a height of about a foot or two above the ground.

Sometimes it is desirable to loft or lob the ball in order to clear it over the opposition or to put a shot for goal above the reach of the goalkeeper. The ball can be lifted by making several small adjustments. First, place the nonkicking foot just behind rather than beside the ball. Then, as you kick, put your instep well under the center of the ball and let both knees straighten with the impact. When properly executed, your body weight is behind rather than over the ball at the moment of contact and your follow-through, which goes almost to waist height, is accompanied by a rise to the toes of the supporting foot.

INSIDE OF THE FOOT KICK (fig. 3). Much of the play in soccer moves the ball laterally as well as forward in order that it may be passed from teammate to teammate or be angled toward the goal. One can easily send the ball at any angle between straight forward and directly sideward by contacting it with the inside of the foot and ankle. The Inside of the Foot Kick is accurate and quick for a short or medium-length pass, but it is not deceptive, for the intended direction is apparent to an observant opponent.

1. Position your supporting foot with the toe just behind and to the side of the ball and pointed toward the target.
2. Swing the kicking leg diagonally forward from the hip, knee slightly flexed, toe turned out, and ankle flexed so that the foot is parallel to the ground.
3. Keep the knees of both legs and the kicking ankle flexed but firm upon impact with the horizontal axis of the ball. Since the ball has continued to roll toward you, it will be beside the supporting foot at impact.
4. Follow through low in the direction of the kick.
5. For a push pass, place the kicking foot and ankle against the ball and shove, keeping both knees and ankles flexed as indicated above.
6. To loft or lob the ball, meet it below center, lifting the kicking foot upon contact and turning up the sole of the foot.

OUTSIDE OF THE FOOT KICK. Although limited in power, this kick is particularly good for short, quick passes between adjacent forwards. It may be done as a push pass, in which case the backswing is omitted.

1. With the toe down and turned in slightly, bring the kicking leg diagonally forward in front of the supporting foot, both knees bent.
2. Swing the kicking leg, straightening the knee as you contact the ball squarely with the outer part of the foot and ankle. Ideally you will meet the ball in line with the shoulder of the kicking leg and just ahead of the supporting foot.

PUNT. The punt is a volley kick in which the ball is contacted after being dropped from the kicker's own hands. For the sake of speed and accuracy, the player should not toss the ball but release it at arm's length to fall vertically. The weight is on the nonkicking foot as the drop is made. One or two preceding steps increase momentum and impart greater force

Figure 3—The Inside of the Foot Kick

Figure 4—The Dribble with the Insides of the Feet

to the kick. If the punter is threatened by an opponent, she should shield the ball with her body and then, if necessary, pivot at the last moment to get herself into proper alignment with the ball.

DRIBBLE (fig. 4). Dribbling is the act of propelling the ball along the ground by a series of short kicks to oneself. The technique is advantageous in maneuvering the ball into a good position for an ensuing play or for retaining possession of the ball when a teammate is not free to receive a pass. It is unwise, however, to dribble in preference to passing unless no opponent is near, for the ball progresses relatively slowly when it must be tapped gently to keep it close to the runner's feet, and the direction the dribbler will take can usually be anticipated by the opposing team. If the dribbler cannot pass when she is about to be tackled, she should use deceptive movements and sudden changes of direction or pace in an effort to evade her opponent.

The insides or outsides of the feet can be used to tap the ball in dribbling. The former method is slower but much the easier for the novice.

Dribbling with the Insides of the Feet

1. Lean forward to keep the body weight over the ball throughout the dribble.
2. Lift one foot several inches above the ground and turn the toe outward.
3. Tap the ball gently with the inner border of the foot. The ball should move forward in a slightly diagonal direction so that it can be tapped next with the other foot.
4. Step forward on the kicking foot.
5. Continue the tap-step pattern with alternate feet while running as rapidly as possible without losing control of the ball. If you have an open field and are a forward line player, you need not tap the ball on every step. A foot pattern of tap-step, step, step, for example, results in a looser dribble but much faster progress. Half-

backs are advised not to adopt this method, however, because of the increased risk of being successfully tackled when the defense is thin behind them. Fullbacks make very little use of the dribble in any form.

Basics of Blocking and Volleying

1. Note that in its elementary form, blocking is a passive method of propulsion. Simply provide a firm surface from which the ball can rebound in the desired direction.
2. If you want to take the speed off the ball, "give" as the ball is met in order to absorb the force of the impact. Incline the contacting body surface so the ball will be directed toward the ground. This kind of blocking is a form of control as well as of propulsion.
3. If you wish to impart force to the rebound, the block becomes a "volley." Move forward to strike the ball with the body.

Blocking With the Shins. A rolling or bouncing ball often can be advanced by letting it strike the shins. It is easier to make an effective block on the up-bounce than on the descent of the ball.

1. With the feet slightly apart and knees easy, align yourself with the approaching ball.
2. Rise on your toes and bend the knees slightly as the ball strikes the shins. Your feet must fully support your body weight, for if you kneel on the ball you are apt to fall.

Thigh Block. When the ball approaches at a suitable height, it may be controlled by meeting it with the inside of the thigh.

1. With the body in line with the oncoming ball, lift the knee of the blocking leg so that the inside of the thigh is at right angles to the path of the ball.
2. As the ball strikes the leg, relax the muscles and withdraw the thigh slightly.

Basics of Throwing

The rules place no restrictions on methods of throwing the ball. The distance of the pass, the locations of other players, and the position in which the ball is caught are factors in the choice of type of throw.

1. Use a one-arm overhand or side-arm throw for distance. These throws, however, tend to lack precision.
2. Use a two-hand overhead, underhand, or chest pass for greater accuracy but shorter distance.
3. Note that the angle of release determines the direction of ball flight.

Chest Pass. This is an accurate method of throwing, useful for short passes. In speedball it makes for a speedy return following a catch at chest height.

1. Hold the ball in two hands at chest height, fingers spread around the sides and pointed upward and thumbs behind. Flex the elbows close to the sides of the body.
2. With the feet in stride position, push the ball forward with the thumbs as you snap your wrists and extend your elbows.

Two-hand Overhead Pass. This short pass is useful in getting the ball above the reach of a guarding opponent in speedball.

1. Hold the ball as for a chest pass but with the arms high and just in front of the head.
2. Bend the elbows and flex the wrists to draw the ball backward to directly above or a little behind the head.
3. Release the ball with a forward swing of the forearms and a strong wrist snap.

Baseball Throw. The ball can be thrown for a considerable distance with this pass. The goalkeeper and speedball backfield players often use it to clear the ball quickly from the goal area.

1. Brace the ball with one hand while letting it rest on the spread fingers and heel of the throwing hand.
2. Rotate the trunk to the throwing side, bring the ball to a position behind the ear, and withdraw the supporting hand.
3. Propel the ball by forcefully extending the elbow and snapping the wrist and pushing the fingers forward behind the ball.

One- or Two-hand Underhand Pass. These passes cover relatively short distances but permit much versatility in the direction of the throw. The backswing can be taken in any direction: backward, sideward, or forward. The release is usually in the direction opposite to the backswing but may be at an angle for deceptive purposes.

1. Hold the ball in both hands with fingers spread on the sides, little fingers behind.
2. Cock the wrists and flex the elbows on the backswing.
3. For a one-hand pass, remove the supporting hand just after you complete the backswing.
4. Straighten the elbows and wrists as you swing the ball in the desired direction of the release.
5. As the ball leaves the hand or hands, push it firmly with the fingers.

Controlling the Ball

Gaining control of an approaching ball implies intercepting it, slowing it down, or stopping it, and bringing it into a position from which it can be propelled effectively. The trunk and legs may be used for fielding the ball. The hands may also be used by the goalkeeper in soccer to catch the ball and by all speedball players when the ball is "aerial."

Almost as challenging as learning to propel the ball with the feet is learning *not* to use the hands for fielding when it is illegal to do so. It will be particularly tempting during the first few days of practice to reach for the ball when doubtful that one's kicking skills are equal to the task. Indeed, the lifelong habit of manipulating objects with the upper extremities is so ingrained that it will require the utmost concentration and diligence to avoid this unconscious reaction under stress. For this reason the novice must learn immediately to control a moving ball without catching it with the hands. This can be done not only by "giving" with the body while blocking but by actually stopping the ball with the feet or legs. This is called "trapping."

It is well at this point to note distinctions among *blocking, volleying,* and *trapping,* since the terms may be confused. If the purpose is to propel the ball, it is blocked by letting it rebound by its own force, or it is volleyed by moving toward the ball to add impetus to the rebound. If the object is to stop the ball, it is trapped by securing it against the ground with one or both feet or legs.

Fielding skills are often neglected by novice players who are apt to dash forward to meet each oncoming ball with the one intention of kicking it back toward the opponents' goal as hard as possible. The result is a confused scramble of players racing back and forth down the field. The kicks are usually wild, sometimes dangerous, and seldom effective in scoring goals. It is difficult to govern direction and force if the ball is not first brought under the control of the receiver.

Basics of Trapping

1. Keep your eyes on the ball.
2. Align yourself so that the desired receiving surface of the body is directly in the path of the approaching ball.
3. If the ball is to be fielded while in the air, angle the receiving surface downward so that the ball will rebound toward the ground.
4. At the moment of contact with the ball, "give" in order to dissipate the force of the impact.
5. When you trap with a foot or leg, make sure body weight is supported entirely by the other foot throughout the action.

   Sole of the Foot Trap (fig. 5). This is the simplest, most used means of fielding rolling or low bouncing balls.
1. Align yourself with the oncoming ball.
2. With your weight on the supporting foot, reach the other foot forward, heel low, sole at a 45° angle and several inches above the ground.
3. If the ball is rolling, let it enter the trap formed by the sole of the foot and the ground.
4. If the ball is bouncing, lift the angled sole of the foot to meet the ball in the air, simultaneously releasing the muscular tension in the trapping

Figure 5—The Sole of the Foot Trap

leg so that it "gives" with the impact, as in catching a hard throw with the hands.

5. With the weight still on the supporting foot, the trapping foot is then free to pass or initiate a dribble.

Inside of the Foot Trap (fig. 6). This trap is a bit more difficult to learn than the sole of the foot technique, but it has two advantages: it is useful for receiving rolling and low bouncing balls approaching from the side as well as from the front, and it finishes with the trapping foot behind the body ready to kick without a preliminary backswing.

1. With your weight on the supporting foot, turn the inside of the trapping foot toward the ball with the sole of the foot 3 to 4 inches off the ground and parallel to it.

2. Keeping both knees slightly bent, reach out to meet the ball with the trapping foot.

3. At the moment of impact, cushion the force by letting the trapping foot move backward with the ball.

Shin Trap (fig. 7). An alternative means of trapping a rolling or bouncing ball coming from the front is by use of the shins. This may be safer than the Sole of the Foot Trap because a larger receiving surface is presented to the ball.

Side of the Leg Trap (fig. 8). This is an easy but slow way to field a rolling ball, recommended only when you are unhurried.

1. With the weight on the supporting foot, turn the body slightly toward the trapping foot.

2. Flex both knees, place the inner border of the trapping foot on the ground at right angles to the path of the ball, and angle the trapping leg knee well toward the ball.

3. Catch the ball between the inner side of the leg and the ground.

Figure 6—The Inside of the Foot Trap

Figure 7—The Shin Trap

Figure 8—The Side of the Leg Trap

Inside of the Legs Trap. This modification of the Shin Trap may seem awkward but it is useful to players who experience difficulty in lowering the shins far enough to hold the ball.

1. Assume a narrow stride in line with the ball, toes turned out slightly and trunk inclined forward.
2. Bend the knees, bringing them close together to form a triangular pocket with the insides of the lower legs and the ground.

Basics of Catching

The goalkeeper in soccer and all speedball players should become adept at fielding with the hands as well as with the feet, legs, and body. Catching is a familiar skill but the rather common tendency to point the fingers at the ball and thus court injury makes a reminder of good form seem advisable.

1. Reach out for the ball, elbows slightly bent.
2. Point the fingers diagonally up and out for balls above the waist and diagonally down and out for balls below the waist.
3. Contact the ball with fingers spread, relaxed, and slightly curved.
4. "Give" with the catch and pull the ball toward the body to absorb the force and secure the catch.

Skills Specific to Speedball

Conversion of a Ground Ball to an Aerial Ball

The conversion of a ground ball to an aerial ball may be done by lifting it to another player or to oneself.

Kick-up with Two Feet to Self (fig. 9)

1. Trap the ball between the feet with the inner borders and ankles touching the ball.
2. Roll your weight to the outer borders of the feet as you flex the knees slightly and bend the trunk a little forward.
3. Jump and flex the knees quickly to lift the ball so that you can catch it.

Figure 9—The Kick-up with Two Feet to Self

Which method of trapping is good if the ball is approaching from the side? Which is good if you find it hard to lower your shins far enough to do a shin trap?

Lift of a Stationary Ball to Another Player
1. With the knees slightly bent and the weight on one foot, place the toe of the other foot under the ball.
2. Flip the ball into the air by straightening the knees as you lift the ball on the instep.

Kick-up of a Moving Ball (fig. 10)
1. Align yourself with the approaching ball with your weight on the supporting foot.
2. If the ball is rolling, extend the other foot, toe down, toward the ball and let the ball roll onto the toe. You can simply let the ball roll on up the leg or you can give the ball an upward impetus with the foot.
3. If the ball is bouncing, bend the knees and meet it with the foot below the horizontal axis. By a gentle upward kick, direct the ball to yourself or to another player.

Figure 10—The Kick-up of a Moving Ball

3 Advanced Techniques

By the time the novice has perfected her ability to perform the standard fundamental soccer techniques, she will have discovered that numerous unorthodox methods of playing the ball are also possible and sometimes necessary. Truly, almost any part of the body can be used to propel or control the ball and the choice of the means becomes an instinctive reaction for the highly skillful player. Nevertheless, there are some recognized techniques which are helpful when learned; they are somewhat difficult but are mechanically functional and tactically sound when used under the proper circumstances. These techniques, usually beyond the needs or capabilities of the novice, give an edge to the player who has practiced enough to master them.

Volley Kick

The decision to volley kick usually is forced on a player by the necessity for quick and decisive action. The descending ball is played before it reaches the ground, thus enabling the kicker to clear over a threatening opponent or try for goal without trapping first. The volley kick is used mostly by fullbacks, since they are anxious not only to break up a rush toward the goal but to return the ball far upfield.

The kick is usually made with the instep, but the contact surface may be the inside, outside, or even the heel of the foot. In any case, the technique is much the same as for playing ground balls except that the body is a little behind rather than over the ball as it is met. If it is desired to loft the ball high, the point of contact is well above the ground and the toe is not kept dropped on the follow-through.

Half-Volley and Drop Kick

The half-volley is a kick in which the instep contacts an aerial ball immediately after it has struck the ground. Like the volley, it can cover long distances and is executed without first trapping the ball. Although some control is thus sacrificed, the speed with which the defense can clear the ball well upfield with it, or the attack can take advantage of an opportunity to shoot for goal, may sometimes be more important. In general, the half-volley flies more horizontally than the volley.

Timing is the most difficult element to master in learning the half-volley. If too early with the leg swing, the kicker probably will "top" the ball before it hits the ground and, if too late, the instep will catch the ball underneath and cause it to rise almost vertically.

The drop kick (fig. 11) is a half-volley which is initiated by dropping the ball from the hands to the ground at arm's length ahead of the body. The drop coincides with a preliminary step forward on the non-kicking foot. If there is no need to clear the ball over the head of an attacker who is close by, goalkeepers may prefer the drop kick to the punt because the lower trajectory will return the ball to the center field area more quickly.

Figure 11—The Drop Kick

Backward Heel Kick

When a player wishes to make a pass-back without taking time to turn around to face the teammate behind her, the backward heel kick is useful.

1. While moving beside the ball, step well ahead of it on the supporting foot.

Can you distinguish between a half volley and a drop kick? If you delay the kick in either of these methods, what is the effect on the ball? What happens if you hurry the kick?

2. Swing the kicking foot forward, straightening the knee and lifting the toes.
3. Swing the kicking leg forcefully backward by flexing the knee and contact the ball squarely with the heel.

Pivot Kick (fig. 12)

When a player is hurried and unable to position herself well, she may have to approach a ground ball at a right angle to the direction she wishes to pass. The pivot kick is the answer, for it is designed to change the ball's direction. The kick also serves as a deceptive ploy, especially on free kicks, corner kicks, and shots for goal.

1. Place the supporting foot about a foot from the ball, with the toe pointing toward the ball.
2. Swing your kicking leg forward as for a regular instep kick while simultaneously pivoting on the ball of the supporting foot to turn the toe in the direction of the intended pass. The right foot must be the kicking foot if you want to kick to the left.
3. Contact the ball with the shoelaces slightly below the horizontal axis of the ball. Carry the body weight well forward throughout the kicking action to avoid losing your balance and in order to give force to the ball.

Figure 12—The Pivot Kick

Spinning Kicks (fig. 13)

The ultimate in control in kicking is achieved by applying "English," or spin to the ball. The principle is simple but accurate execution is difficult. A ball with English follows an arc that curves in the direction of the spin. Top spin brings a ball to the ground fast or holds it on the ground, whereas back spin lofts the ball. Lateral spin causes the ball to follow a path that curves to the right or left.

Path of Ball
and
Direction of Spin

1. For top spin, contact the ball slightly above center and keep the follow-through low.
2. For back spin, meet the ball slightly below center and follow-through high.
3. For lateral spin, strike the ball just to the side of center and follow-through as if brushing the foot along the side of the ball.

Figure 13—The Points of Contact for Spinning Kicks

Dribbling With Outside of Foot

Mastery of this technique adds greater speed and versatility to the basic form of dribbling. If one foot is used, the ball need be contacted only on every second or fourth stride, thus allowing a faster run. When outsides and insides of the feet are used in combination, the player can easily move in an arc rather than in a straight line. The only significant difference between the two forms of the dribble is that the foot is turned out slightly for the Inside of the Foot Dribble and is rotated inward for the Outside of the Foot Dribble.

Heading (fig. 14)

Propelling an aerial ball by intercepting it with the head is a very useful means of controlling the play when the ball is descending from above. Attackers find heading particularly effective in scoring goals and, conversely, defenders can deflect a high ball from the danger area more quickly by heading than by waiting to meet the ball with a lower part of the body.

Heading is not an uncomfortable skill to perform when properly executed, but it looks difficult and even frightening to the novice. To gain confidence, it is essential to understand exactly what is to be done before trying to play the ball in this manner and then to practice assiduously until timing and accuracy are perfected. During the early stages of learning, the ball may be slightly deflated in order to make the impact easy.

The key to success is to move to meet the ball rather than to wait for it to strike. The hairline at the center of the forehead is the point of contact if the ball is to be sent in a forward direction. If the ball is to be passed at an angle, contact is made just above the temple. The player may jump from one or both feet to reach the ball at the earliest moment or, if

Figure 14—Heading

time permits, she can wait in a forward stride position with knees bent. In the latter, the straightening of the knee of the rear leg begins just prior to contact. Regardless of preliminary position, the tensing of the neck muscles and the movement of the body toward the ball provide force and thus speed of rebound equal to that gained from many kicks.

Split Tackle

When all else fails and it is imperative to dislodge the ball from the opponent's control, a split tackle may offer the only solution. This is a last-resort move because the tackler is not left in a position either to make a second try if she fails or to dribble if she succeeds.

1. Approach the opponent from the side or from the front.
2. Place your feet in an easy stride position and incline the trunk slightly forward.
3. As the ball leaves the opponent's foot, drop to one knee and simultaneously thrust your other leg at the ball and lean away from the ball. Your reach will be maximum if you contact the ball with the toe of your shoe.

Blocking With the Abdomen, Chest, or Shoulder

Fly balls coming at appropriate heights may be blocked with the shoulder, or with the arms, *provided they are held in contact with the body.* When blocking with the abdomen (fig. 15), firmly contract the muscles to avoid discomfort when the ball strikes. The "give" necessary if the action is to precede a trap must come from a "caving-in" movement of the trunk as you contact the ball. A chest block is in order when balls approach from the front and at a higher level. As the ball nears, each hand firmly grasps the opposite upper are and the elbows are pressed snugly against the body in order to protect the chest and to avoid an illegal play. The same arm position, although not necessary for safety, may help by ensuring that the upper arm remains still and against the body when contacting balls with the shoulder. If the receiver's intention is to use a chest block as a pass, she should move toward the ball to impart force to the rebound.

Figure 15—Blocking with the Abdomen

Hook Pass

The hook pass is effective when actively guarded because the passer can interpose her body between her throwing arm and the opponent. The timing and control of the pass are difficult, however, especially if the passer's hand is too small to hold the ball securely.

1. Holding the ball at waist height, use one hand to wedge the ball between the other forearm and hand.
2. Take a full arm swing carrying the ball back behind the shoulder as you turn your other side toward the target.
3. Continue the arm swing through an upward arc to the point of release, which is overhead.
4. Flex the elbow, snap the wrist, and push with the finger tips at the moment of release.

Snap Kick-up to Self (Specific to Speedball)

1. With your weight on the supporting foot, place the sole of the other foot on top of the stationary ball.
2. Draw the foot toward the body, quickly tuck the toe under the ball, and lift the knee and toe as if picking up a tennis ball on a racket.

4 Patterns of Play

Team play begins with the allocation of duties to each of the eleven players. Both offensive and defensive responsibilities fall to everyone but, generally speaking, these are distributed on a graduated scale from the backfield to the forward line with the goalkeeper playing *most* defensively and the forwards most offensively. Various means of propelling and controlling the ball or moving about the field are employed for specific purposes. These actions are called individual tactics if performed by one player, team tactics when two or more teammates cooperate in the maneuvers. The final component of teamwork is strategy, which can be thought of as the master plan, the patterning of the play of the entire team.

Position Play in Soccer

Goalkeeper

The goalkeeper's three primary functions are to prevent goals, to shift her team's play from defense to offense, and to direct the actions of the fullbacks and halfbacks. Accomplishment of these purposes requires speed and agility, superior timing, courage, initiative, and acute awareness of the developing patterns of play.

Unlike her teammates, the goalkeeper is armed with special privileges inside the penalty area which permit her to handle the ball. She may pick up the ball, bounce it once, throw it, drop kick or punt it, combine the bounce with a throw or kick, or take two steps instead of a bounce. She should exploit these privileges whenever possible; for the most effective and fastest way to clear the goal area, if the situation allows it, is to catch the ball, step to the side of the goal with it, and then throw to a teammate.

The goalkeeper's basic waiting position is about three feet in front of the center of the goal line (fig. 16). From here she shifts laterally to the side on which the ball is being played in order to narrow the space through which the ball can cross between the goal posts without strong probability of her interception. Should a free ball or a single opponent approach when a fullback cannot intercept, the goalkeeper must move forward at once to attack. She should be wary, however, of leaving the near vicinity of the goal unless a fullback can step in to cover.

A cardinal rule of goalkeeping is to keep as much body surface as possible between the ball and the goal. When catching an aerial ball, the

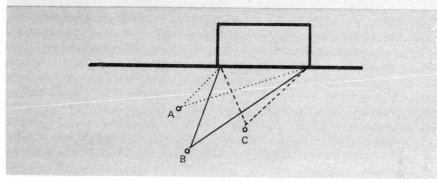

SHOOTING ANGLES
Which position, A, B, or C, affords the attacker the greatest margin for error in her shot for goal? Should the goalkeeper move to her own left of center to defend against a shot from A? Which shot is easiest to block?

Figure 16—The Goalkeeper on Guard

trunk becomes a secondary line of defense if the catch is fumbled. Similarly, if the heels are held together and the toes turned out, a ground ball missed by the hands may be blocked. Should the ball be bouncing, a drop to one knee will place a good barrier behind the catch. A second cardinal rule is to get the ball immediately from the center to one side of the goal and then to pass it to a teammate, preferably the wing on the same side of the field. *Never* pass the ball across the goal mouth for fear of interception.

The drop kick and the punt are the best alternatives to a hard throw by the goalkeeper but she should also be prepared to tip a high ball over the crossbar, or to punch, head, block, or volley-kick the ball if there is not opportunity to field the ball prior to clearing it.

The goalkeeper directs the play of the fullbacks and sometimes the halfbacks by calling to them. She warns them of unguarded opponents and advises them to close in, stay back, or shift position.

Fullbacks

The duties of the fullbacks are primarily defensive, that is, to work closely with the goalkeeper to protect the goal and, better yet, with the halfbacks to prevent the ball from entering their end of the field. The fullbacks also mark the inners on their respective sides of the field and usually are called upon to take defense kicks. Despite this emphasis on defense, if opportunity arises to carry the attack, there should be no hesitation in so doing. In this case a halfback should drop back to cover the fullback's position.

Particularly valuable are the volley and half-volley kicks, heading, and other forms of blocking, for the fullbacks should pass the ball upfield as quickly as possible and under the pressure of attack often have no chance even to drop the ball first.

A shifting diagonal relationship, in which the fullback on the side of the field where the ball is moves forward and the other fullback drops back and toward the center, provides defensive depth. The fullbacks should stay between their opponents and the goal and give priority to jockeying an attacker toward the side line rather than tackling at the risk of being passed by the opponent. The fullbacks should never send the ball across the front of the goal mouth but neither should they lose sight of the advantage which is sometimes to be gained by passing back to the goalkeeper, who is privileged to use her hands on the ball.

The general area of play is from the goal line to the center field. Each fullback covers her own side, but there is overlap in the middle across the mouth of the goal (fig. 17).

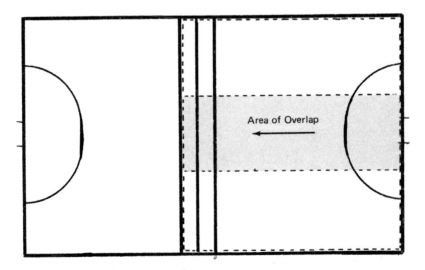

Figure 17—Areas of Play for Soccer Fullbacks

Halfbacks (fig. 18)

As their team advances and retreats, the halfbacks change roles. Their responsibilities range from goal defense to scoring tries and their repertory of skills must be equal to the challenge. Endurance, too, is very important, for the halfbacks must be in constant motion in order to serve as the connecting link between the forward line and the fullbacks. On attack, the halfbacks play approximately 4 to 6 yards behind the forwards in readiness to receive and return passes, to take free kicks, or to mark and tackle opponents who try to interfere with the team's advance. On defense, the side halfbacks mark their respective wings and the center marks the center forward.

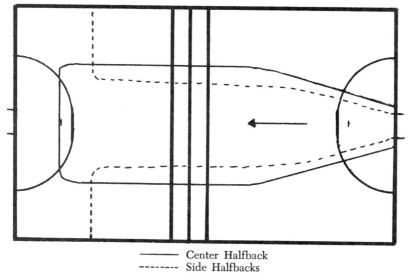

——————— Center Halfback
- - - - - - - - Side Halfbacks

Figure 18—Areas of Play for Soccer Halfbacks

The Center Halfback. At advanced levels of competition, the center halfback functions mostly as a defensive player in the position of a third fullback. It is easier and more advisable at the elementary stages, however, for her to limit herself to the usual halfback responsibilities, which are demanding enough in themselves.

An ability to receive and to pass well—both to the left and the right—in order to spread the play and to change its direction quickly is important. Because the play and the players tend to concentrate lengthwise in the central third of the field, mistakes in judgment and inaccuracies in passing by the center half are sometimes concealed by the rapidity of the action in that area. There is danger that the center half will feel she has been effective if she has been able to kick the ball somehow, no matter in which direction or with what force. To guard against this false security, the center half must scan the peripheral areas constantly so that her passes are preplanned to reach teammates who are advantageously situated.

The center halfback marks the center forward on a man-to-man basis unless the forward roams toward the side of the field. In that event, it is advisable for the halfback to remain in her normal zone of play so that there will never be an unprotected opening in front of the goal.

Left and Right Halfbacks. These players position themselves to the left and right of the center halfback and behind the inside forwards. As the ball approaches the opponents' penalty area, these halfbacks often assist in sending the ball to the center, for that location generally offers possibilities for successful attempts at scoring. This is not to imply, however, that halfbacks should pass up a good opportunity to shoot for goal.

Defensively, the side halfbacks mark the opposing wings, but as players shift laterally they may also be called upon to tackle the center forward or the inners. Every effort should be made to force opponents toward the side lines.

When the ball is sent out of bounds over the side line, the throw-in is customarily taken by the halfback on that side of the field. She should move quickly to put the ball into play again before the opponents can get into position to intercept. Usually the throw-in is directed to the nearer wing or the inside forward. The halfback throws and immediately runs onto the field in readiness to receive a passback, to back up the ball's advance, or to tackle if an opponent gains its possession.

Forwards (fig. 19)

Attack and scoring goals are the chief activities of the five forwards, but they also form the first line of defense and must be ready to mark their respective opponents and to tackle as the need arises. The opponents whom they mark are the same ones who in reverse mark them; for example, the left wing marks the opposite right halfback. Forwards must possess the speed necessary to keep up with the ball and, if possible, to outdistance their opponents. Short diagonal passes to an adjacent teammate and occasionally back to a halfback are most effective when interspersed now and then with long crossfield plays to unbalance the defense. Forwards have the opportunity to dribble more than their teammates do but, like them, should elect to pass as soon as there is an opening.

Center Forward. With the central portion of the field as her usual area of play, the center forward probably will be the team's principal scorer. As such, she must be adept at receiving passes from the right or left and at shooting for the goal, often without opportunity to trap the ball first. In her haste, however, she should not overlook the possibility that a pass to an inside forward, a wing, or a halfback may open a better scoring opportunity than if she had made the try herself.

The center forward always takes the kick-off and often the penalty kick. Both tasks require accurate control of a place kick, including the ability to loft it or keep it on the ground at will. Both situations also permit set plays in which she and her teammates are prepared to follow up the kick in a preplanned fashion.

Inners. Triangular passing among three adjacent forwards, or among two adjacent forwards and a halfback, of necessity includes an inside for-

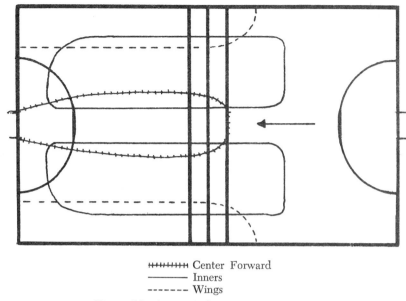

HHHHHHH Center Forward
——————— Inners
------- Wings

Figure 19—Areas of Play for Soccer Forwards

ward. Situated as they are, the inners can be thought of as the middlemen of the attack. This hub position brings responsibility for relaying passes to and from the center and wing forwards and the halfbacks. This middleman role is strenuous, for the ball is often within the province of the inners and they must be ready to receive and pass off either side.

Not only do the inside forwards take the brunt of carrying the ball down the field, but their hub position away from the opponents' defense also gives them the power to distribute the play. Their team's offense depends heavily on them to find and to open holes in the defense. When an inner has the ball she can set up an attacking maneuver by quickly redirecting the ball to take advantage of a space through which to drive. If she is not in possession of the ball, she may be able to accomplish the same thing by moving in such a way as to draw her opponent away from the ball or out of a good covering position.

Defensively, the first task of the inside forwards is to cover their respective side fullbacks. The inners may tackle or, perhaps better, may engage in a delaying action that will give their own defense time to form behind the ball. As the opponents approach within striking distance of the goal, the defensive inners should move in toward the center, ready to clear the ball to a wing.

Wings. By tradition based on sound reasons, the wings are speedy runners who cannot only keep up with the ball but get ahead of it. They are expected to dribble at a rapid pace and to receive and pass accurately on the run. Normally the wings also take corner kicks. The play of the wings is more concentrated on the side away from the sideline. It is advantageous, therefore, for the left wing to be left-footed and vice versa.

Typically, a team tries to get the ball out to a wing who then works in conjunction with the inside and center forwards and the side halfback to advance the ball by means of triangular passing and dribbling. As the goal area is approached, the wing passes to the center forward, who shoots. However, the wings, in the interest of deceptive strategy, must avoid sameness in their play by departing from this pattern. Long, crossfield passes or interchanges with the inner can sometimes throw opponents off guard.

The wings have fewer opportunities to shoot than the centrally located forwards, but if they react quickly to openings in the defense, there will be times when they can move in to attack the goal personally. When they cannot, they set up the thrust for goal by wise placement and choice of height of the centering kick to another forward. If the wing can advance far enough toward the goal line to get off a pass that travels behind the defenders to the inside or center forward, there will be little chance of interception. Caution is required, however, to avoid being trapped by a concentrated defense. Once the attacking play is in front of the goal and centered between the side lines, the wings may drop back toward their own goal line to help their backfield teammates cover clearing kicks by the defense. On the other hand, when a team's own goal is threatened, the wings may move away from the goal line to position themselves to receive clearing kicks by their teammates.

Position Play in Speedball

Position play, individual and team tactics, and strategy in speedball and soccer are very similar and the speedball player should be guided by the descriptions of these aspects of the game on pages 22-28, 30- 34, and 36-40. (Good pointers can be found also in *Field Hockey* by Anne L. Delano, one of the William C. Brown Company Physical Education Activities Series.) Nevertheless, the aerial play, the touchdown and drop kick methods of scoring, and the lack of an offside rule in speedball make for several important differences in the patterns of play.

Position Play

The *Goalkeeper's* role in speedball is the same as in soccer except that in Speedball she must be ready to defend against more fly balls. Height is thus a major asset to this player. The goalkeeper should not take responsibility for the prevention of touchdowns; the area between the goal posts is her only concern.

The *fullbacks* function much as they do in soccer, primarily as defense players but sometimes participating in the ground or aerial attack. Balls sent out of bounds over the goal line by the offensive team are often returned to play by the nearer fullback, who should move quickly to the end line before the opponents can get set to intercept. The fullbacks also are responsible for defending against touchdown tries near the goal. They should, however, avoid being drawn toward the side lines when they are deep in their backfield, for this would leave the goalkeeper without good support (fig. 20).

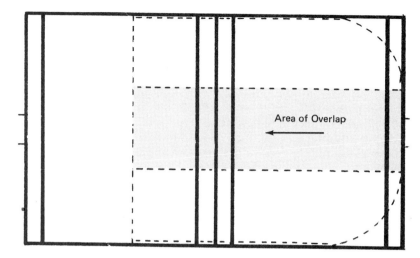

Figure 20—Areas of Play for Speedball Fullbacks

The *halfbacks'* duties differ noticeably in soccer and speedball. Because the touchdown is much used for scoring, play near the goal line tends to remain spread across the field, rather than becoming centered in front of the goal mouth (fig. 21). Much of the defense against touchdown tries falls to the three halfbacks, and when their team is attacking they are often in position to make the touchdown pass or to drop kick for a goal. Occasionally a halfback may cross the end line to receive a touchdown pass

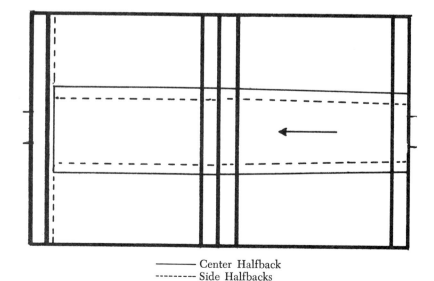

——————— Center Halfback
- - - - - - - - Side Halfbacks

Figure 21—Areas of Play for Speedball Halfbacks

as a surprise tactic. The center halfback in speedball does *not* function mostly as a defensive player at advanced levels of competition as she does in soccer. Instead, she takes a very active role in offensive play.

The *forwards* (fig. 22) lead the attack, both on the ground and in the air. They should be ready to shift in an instant from one form of play to the other in order to seize openings and disconcert opponents. Forwards should be particularly adept at aerial passing and man-to-man guarding and should make full use of basketball type screen plays and feints. They should take advantage of the lack of an offside rule in speedball by moving ahead of the play to receive passes. A great premium is played on speed for the wing positions, since these players have the greatest lengthwise distance to cover.

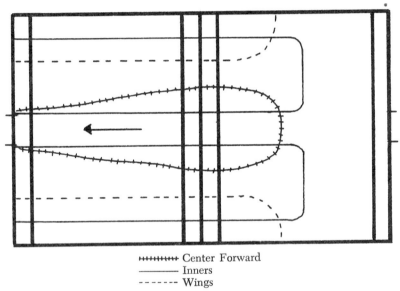

                     ┼┼┼┼┼┼┼ Center Forward
                     ────── Inners
                     ------ Wings

Figure 22—Areas of Play for Speedball Forwards

Individual Offensive
and Defensive Tactics

The team in possession of the ball is the attacking team, regardless of where the ball is being played at the moment. Individual tactics which the attackers can employ include passing, shooting, feinting, dodging, drawing, and body blocking. For all of these offensive tactics, there are counteractions which may succeed in taking the ball away from the attacking team. Defensive tactics include marking, tackling, covering, and drawing, the last of which is also used by the attack.

Passing

The purpose of a pass is to send the ball to its target accurately, speedily, and without interception. The ball may be **propelled** by any legal means and may proceed on the ground or in the air. A pass should be directed to an open space which the passer judges can be reached by the teammate in time to receive the ball. The sender should not follow her pass but, instead, should seek a position where she will be free to receive a return pass. When to pass depends upon the situation of the moment, but in general it is as soon as possible. A pass may be delayed by dribbling if the player has a clear field ahead, if she wishes to pull an opponent out of position, or if no receiver is free. If there is an option, it is unwise to delay a pass when deep in one's own half of the field or if the ball has just been obtained by tackling an opponent.

Evading An Opponent

The team with the ball has three means of evading an opponent: by outnumbering her, by outmaneuvering her, and by deceptive motions which are called "feints."

A feint is intended to mislead the opponent into making the wrong move. It may be accomplished by gestures with any part of the body, by stepping in a false direction, or even by looking where the player does *not* plan to go. Feinting must be done convincingly if it is to work and it must not be overdone. When perfected and used in combination with other evasive tactics, it is a most valuable supplementary skill.

There is no way to deal satisfactorily with more than one adversary at once, so the safest means of evading an opponent is to outnumber her by eliciting the aid of a teammate. Any of the following two-man plays, especially if preceded by a feint, may make it possible to escape an opponent:

1. Loft the ball over the head of the opponent to your teammate.
2. Pass straight ahead and, as your teammate moves into your territory to receive the ball, exchange positions with her.
3. Pass to an adjacent teammate and then run by the opponent to receive a return pass.

If there is no teammate able to help, the player in possession of the ball must try to dodge her opponent. Here, too, the feint may contribute to success in the following maneuvers:

1. As you and the opponent approach head-on, take a sudden sidestep to the right just as she steps onto her left foot. Immediately push off with the right foot and make your dodge to your own left. (The play can be done with the reverse foot pattern.)
2. Make a feint to the right side of a head-on attacker. Immediately kick the ball forward past her left side and run by her right side to pick up your own pass.
3. With an opponent at or approaching your side, stop the ball suddenly by placing your foot on top of it, being careful not to transfer any body weight to the trapping foot.

Body Blocking

The player with the ball body blocks when she shields the ball by placing her body between it and the opponent. This tactic may be combined to good advantage with other evasive actions. A player without the ball should be alert to the possibility of body blocking for a teammate by screening away an opponent who might otherwise tackle or intercept a pass.

Marking

The defense against passes of the attacking team is to mark (guard) the player with the ball and those of her teammates who are potential receivers of a pass. "Marking" means to keep an eye on the player for whom one is responsible and to play near enough to tackle her or to intercept passes to her. The defender must size up her opponent's strengths and weaknesses and her style of play in order to judge how closely she must be guarded. The marker tries to stay between her opponent and the goal and attempts to edge the opponent in the direction she wishes her to take.

Tackling

Tackling is an attempt to take the ball away from a player. Success depends not only on a good technique but on precise timing. The ball should be tackled just before the dribbler taps it or passes it, for at that moment she is committed to the action she has begun and cannot dodge. Too early a move to tackle gives the dribbler warning and a chance to use evasive tactics; too late a move finds the tackler reaching for empty air. In any tackle, the body weight should be forward over the ball as the try is made so that if the tackle is successful the tackler will be in a position to play the ball immediately.

Front Tackle (fig. 23)
1. Approach the dribbler head-on.
2. Extend the leg to stop the ball with the sole of the foot. Preferably, the foot is the same as the one the dribbler is about to use to kick the ball.

Hook Tackle (fig. 24)
1. Approach the dribbler head-on and slightly to one side.
2. Extend the leg and hook the ball toward you with the foot nearer the opponent.

Side Tackle (fig. 25)
1. Approach the dribbler from the side or rear.
2. While moving beside her, swing the nearer leg to tap the ball sideways with the outside of the foot.
3. Immediately cross behind the dribbler to pick up the ball, unless a teammate is there to take over for you.

Interchange

Trading places with a teammate is called "interchange" and is a most valuable offensive and defensive tactic. Switching positions occurs when

Figure 23—The Front Tackle

Figure 24—The Hook Tackle

Figure 25—The Side Tackle

a player finds it advantageous to leave the area where she would normally be found. As soon as play permits, the players resume their normal horizontal and longitudinal relationships. The possibility of interchange should not be considered a license to roam freely. The tactic should be employed intentionally because of the necessities of the moment or as a deliberate attempt to confuse the defense. Interchange is not recommended in the early learning stages for it is difficult enough at that point for players to maintain their positions, let alone try to shift from one area to another without bunching.

Drawing

Drawing is causing an opponent to move out of an area. It is both an offensive and a defensive tactic and is a form of evasive action. A player with or without the ball simply moves away from the space she wishes to free and, if the gambit is successful, the marking opponent also shifts her position. The object is to clear a path for a pass or for a shot at the goal. Defense players deep in their territory should not risk waiting to draw an opponent before passing.

Covering

Covering is, in a sense, the opposite of drawing in that it refers to filling a space. A player without the ball covers when she places herself in a pathway through which a pass or shot might be sent. This is an important tactic not only for backfield players but for forwards when their team is on the defense.

Shooting

A shot for a field goal should be made as soon as the ball comes within scoring range, provided the player is not too well guarded. It is essential to observe the positions of the defending players and to aim accordingly before kicking or heading. Ground balls to the low goal corners and lofted or headed balls to the high corners are most likely to get past the goalkeeper. As soon as a shot has been kicked, the kicker and an adjacent forward should rush the goal without waiting to see whether the shot will score. If it does not, the rush forward will give the forwards a good chance for another try at a deflected ball or a chance to block a clearing kick. The forward who accompanies the kicker is the one nearest to the spot where the ball is expected to cross the goal line.

Individual Offensive
and Defensive Tactics for Speedball

The individual tactics employed in soccer (described previously) are equally suitable for speedball when the ball is on the ground and, in most cases, when it is aerial. "Throwing and catching" should be substituted for "kicking or passing and receiving" in aerial play. Two important differences between ground and aerial tactics should be considered, however. First, there is no aerial play in speedball truly comparable to the foot dribble. The aerial dribble is one throw and catch, after which the ball must leave the player's possession. Second, a player can evade a guard and retain possession of the ball in speedball only by taking one step or one air dribble, and so cannot cover much distance without passing.

Guarding in Aerial Play

When an opponent holds the ball, the player responsible for marking should try to gain possession of the ball or should try to prevent a successful pass by guarding in basketball fashion.
1. Lower the center of gravity and widen the base by taking a stride position, slightly crouched, and with the knees easy for good balance and quick changes of direction.
2. Keep two or three feet from your opponent and between her and her potential receiver or the goal.
3. Use the arms in any plane, shifting them as the ball shifts, to block the space through which the opponent wishes to pass.
4. Play the ball, not the person. Try to take the ball out of the hands of your opponent; to tie the ball by placing one or both hands on it firmly; or to intercept the pass.

When an opponent does not have the ball, she is guarded more loosely but in the same manner, except that the arms are not much involved until there is a chance to intercept.
1. Maintain a position between the opponent and your goal in readiness to step forward to intercept a ball coming to her.
2. Watch the opponent's feet and eyes for clues as to her intended direction of movement.
3. If the chance of interception is poor, do not try to do so; instead, move in to guard more closely from a position between your opponent and the potential target for her pass.

Passing By Throwing

Whether a pass is an aerial or a ground tactic, the purpose and governing principles are the same. (see p. 30-31). Specific hints for throwing include:
1. Send a lead pass to a moving teammate.
2. Whenever feasible, aim to chest height.
3. Pass to the nonopponent side of the receiver.
4. Use deceptive moves if necessary to confuse your guard.
5. Use your free arm and your body to keep your guard from closing in when you are going to make a one-hand throw.

Evading an Opponent By Use of an Air Dribble

There is no technique in speedball by which the player holding the ball can dodge her opponent and then continue down the field with the ball still in her possession. It is, however, possible to evade an attacker and cover a short distance in the process by means of the air dribble.

1. Use the free arm and your body to shield the throwing arm from your guard.
2. Loop the ball high enough that it cannot be reached by the guard but not so high that she has time to retrieve it.
3. Use the air dribble to gain time if a receiver is not free. In general, however, a pass is a better tactic.

Team Offensive and Defensive Tactics

Team tactics are those performed through the cooperative actions of members of the attacking or defending team. The tactics may be employed as general procedure or under the particular circumstances of a given play. Such plays as the kick-off, throw-in and free kick in either soccer or speedball; the defense kick and corner kick in soccer (fig. 26); and the toss-up and free throw in speedball afford opportunity for team members to plan ahead and practice specific preplanned tactics, thereby gaining an advantage over the opponents by knowing what is to happen.

Those who have played field hockey, soccer, and speedball will find the offensive and defensive tactics of the sports much alike and therefore interchangeable.

1. Keep the opponents' defense spread thin by carrying the ball along the side lines until striking distance of the goal is approached.
2. Narrow and deepen your own defense as much as possible.
3. Center ground balls near the goal for the best shooting angles.
4. Effect an interchange when necessary to cover for a teammate or when you can gain an advantage by moving into her area.
5. Back up both teammates with the ball and their potential receivers.
6. Vary plays on the kick-off, throw-in, and other set situations so that opponents cannot anticipate the action.
7. Switch the play from side to side of the field.

Strategy

Able as each may be in ball handling and individual tactics, eleven players become a team only when their efforts are coordinated to supplement, reinforce, and replace one another. Strategy—that is, the major purposes and overall plan of operation—is the directive agent which unifies and coordinates a team's performance.

Encompassed in the blanket term "strategy" is the assignment of the territory to be covered by each player. Also included are the method of guarding, zone or man-to-man defense, and the mode of operation for given circumstances. Set plays worked out and practiced in advance may be incorporated into the overall plan.

Field Coverage

A basic horizontal and lengthwise relationship among the team members' playing areas is essential for both offensive and defensive field cov-

Figure 26—Typical Line-up for Soccer Corner Kick

erage. In attacking, maintenance of the basic relationships ensures that the player with the ball can count on finding a potential receiver in a given location. Also, the offense can be spread so as to thin the defense, and play can be shifted at any moment from one side to the other. In defending, the basic relationship can be seen in figure 27, in which imaginary lines have been drawn to provide a "home lane" for each team member. The lane is narrower than any player's full area of responsibility and there is, of course, latitude in respect to where an individual should go. Nevertheless, she should move out of her "home lane" with full awareness of having done so and with cognizance of the desirability of returning as soon as possible. Novice players are advised to hold strictly to basic positions until they are experienced enough to have developed a good "team sense."

Longitudinally, the basic positions for the attack or defense are forwards ahead, halfbacks next, fullbacks behind halves, and last the goalkeeper.

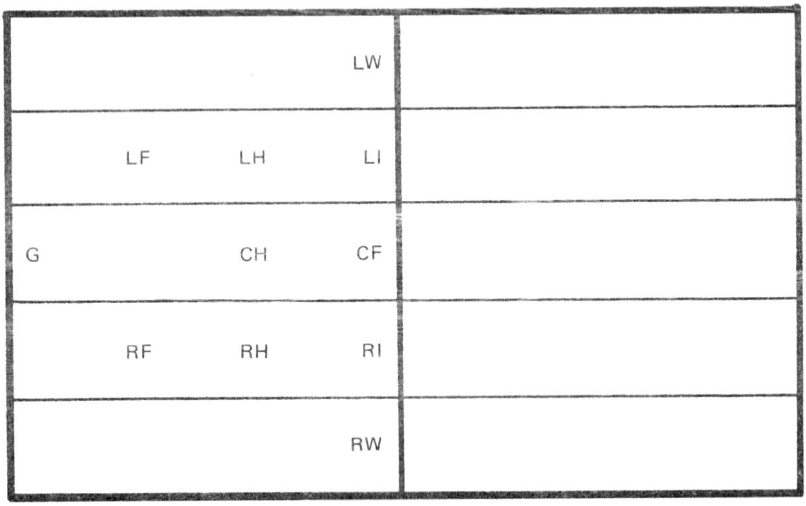

			LW	
	LF	LH	LI	
G		CH	CF	
	RF	RH	RI	
			RW	

Figure 27—Home Lanes for Players

Strategy of the Offense

The offense should shift its formations frequently in accordance with the play and to confuse opponents, but a sound pattern from which to begin is one in which the forwards move in "W" formation and the backfield follows in "M" formation, as shown in figure 28. This zigzag positioning creates diagonal passing lines from player to player. It also makes full use of the breadth of the field, which tends to draw the defense away from the imaginary middle lane.

The play of the offense may be based on short triangular passes, usually among two adjacent forwards and a halfback, or long passes sent

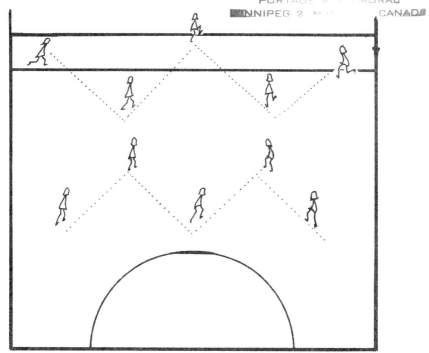

Figure 28—Offensive Team Positions

diagonally across the field. Short, quick passes make for more deceptive play with reduced danger of interception. Progress down the field is slower, however, so that defenders have time to position themselves to protect the goal. The long passing game may catch opponents off guard as the action shifts suddenly to a far distant location. When time is running short, the long passing game is particularly useful, since much yardage is covered in a minimum amount of time. All factors considered and under normal conditions, the short passing style of play interspersed occasionally with long passes is to be preferred. Better ball control is encouraged and the natural tendency of novices to kick hard without careful aim is curbed.

Strategy of the Defense

The best choice of a defense system is a combination of man-to-man and zone guarding. The player marks and tackles her specific opponent wherever she may be in man-to-man defense, whereas in zone defense the defender protects an area by challenging any attacker who enters it.

The strength in man-to-man marking lies in the fact that duties are clear-cut and each adversary is covered. Long crossfield passes by the offense probably will not disconcert the defending team, for each potential receiver is marked. Should a highly skillful attacker be pitted against a weak defender by this usual pattern of assigning responsibilities, it is easy under the man-to-man system to delegate the marking task to a better qualified defender. The weakness of man-to-man guarding is apparent as soon as the attacker strays from her own territory. This may, and probably will if it is done intentionally, draw the defense out of position, thus opening a hole for the attack to break through. Such a hole near the penalty area seriously jeopardizes the defending team's ability to prevent a score.

On the contrary, in zone defense the defenders can situate themselves in the positions they think most effective without having to follow individual opponents. Coverage for each area of the field is thereby provided and individual defenders can converge within the penalty area, the more closely to guard the approaches to the goal. Problems do arise in zone defense when two or more offensive players enter the same area, for someone is bound to be left free to pass or receive. Nevertheless, inexperienced teams are advised to play zone defense because it encourages team members to play their own positions rather than rove, and by so remaining in position they preserve the basic horizontal and longitudinal field coverage relationships.

When man-to-man and zone play are combined the system is more flexible, more complicated—and more effective than either type of defense alone. One combination plan calls for man-to-man defense until the attacking team is within striking distance of the goal. At that time the defensive players converge to form a funnel which narrows toward the goal mouth. Each defender is responsible for covering shots and for marking opponents in her area. The funnel rotates to the left or right, with the goal center as the fulcrum, and thereby provides defense depth for attack from any angle. An alternative combination man-to-man and zone defense play requires that the defenders be basically responsible for their own territories. Wherever the attackers may be, the nearest defenders take them on in man-to-man fashion. An offensive player without the ball is marked loosely when she is within the area of her opponent, but the player with the ball is marked closely.

Speedball Strategy

Speedball strategy incorporates many of the elements of soccer strategy, but differs when the ball is in aerial play. In general, the lateral relationships among the team positions are maintained more consistently in speedball. Centering the ball so as to get into a good scoring position is not so necessary in this sport and, in fact, a well-spread offense carried all the way to the penalty area offers the best possibilities for all forms of scoring. This does not negate the possibility of interchange of forwards as a surprise maneuver, but novices find such a tactic confusing. The lengthwise playing areas for the positions in speedball are increased over the usual soccer limitations since forwards share more defense duties and halfbacks and fullbacks more offense duties, than in soccer (see figs. 20-22, pp. 29-30).

The formation for attack can best be described as a shifting zig-zag in which the thrust to advance continually spearheads at a different point. For maximum effectiveness in an aerial attack, a teammate should speed beyond the player who is about to receive the ball. Ideally, each pass then is in a forward direction, thus ensuring fast progress toward the goal line. When the attack originates with a side player, the forwards may move ahead consecutively so that the temporary pattern becomes a single diagonal line. Usually such a line soon reverts to the more broken zig-zag, owing to the defensive plays of the opponents.

Regardless of whether the forwards are positioned in a V, or W, or in a diagonal line, the player with the ball should be closely followed by a backfield player. Since the player in possession of the ball cannot dribble down the field, she depends primarily on passes to advance the ball. When guarded, a short backward pass is often necessary. Backing-up responsibilities are allotted to the appropriate teammate as in soccer.

Short diagonal aerial passes are strategically sound, for a thrown ball travels more slowly than one which is kicked, and a long throw is often intercepted. Players should not hesitate to drop the ball when a ground opening appears or when the defensive team may be caught off guard by such an action. Actually, the full potential of speedball can be realized only if play is reasonably distributed between ground and aerial play. Novices who are more familiar with throwing than kicking skills tend to convert the ball at every opportunity, thus narrowing the range of offensive tactics, to the detriment of the sport. Aerial play should predominate but never exclude ground action.

Strategy of the Defense

A combination of zone and man-to-man defense is the most efficient and effective system yet devised. Because the offense in speedball remains spread across the field even in the penalty area, the defenders cannot so easily converge around one danger point as in soccer; indeed, the entire breadth of the field is a danger zone.

While the ball is moving down the field, defense coverage will be best under the zone system, whether the play is ground or aerial. One very workable method as the ball approaches the penalty area is for the fullbacks to draw close to the goal mouth in order to assist the goalkeeper in guarding the opening and to cover potential receivers who drop behind the goal line near the goal posts. The defending halfbacks switch to man-to-man guarding of the attacking inners and center forward. Since the attacking halfbacks and wings also present a scoring threat, the defending forwards must join the defense effort. The center forward marks the opposing center half to prevent any attempt on her part to drop kick or send a touchdown pass. The defending inners cover the side halfbacks for the same purpose and the wings take on the opposing wings. The latter seldom drop kick, but since the receiver of a touchdown pass must be behind the goal line, the wings must be prepared to go the same distance and to regain their normal forward line positions rapidly as their team shifts to the attack.

Strategy for Soccer and Speedball Under
Special Playing Conditions

Weather conditions, light, and the playing field surface are considerations in mapping team strategy. When there is a strong wind or a cross wind, clearing kicks from the backfield should be low if into the wind and high if with the wind in order to reduce the impeding effect in the former instance and to carry the ball farther in the latter. When the light comes from one end of the field, send high flying balls so opponents must meet them facing the sun, and low balls to teammates under the same circumstances. The condition of the field surface affects both footing and ball action. The ball is hard to control when the field is wet and slippery and players must cut down running speed. Passers should aim close to receivers and send the ball with less force.

Usually a team prefers to play under adverse conditions during the first half of the game rather than the second, or during the first and third quarters rather than during the second and fourth. Before the coin toss preliminary to starting play, each captain should have looked over the field, made an estimate of the location of the sun during the progress of the game, and considered whether the field surface is apt to improve or deteriorate. The winner of the toss must weigh the combination of the influencing factors against the desirability of kicking off first in the first or last quarter.

Speeding up Progress 5

Soccer and speedball are demanding sports in which the timid, the tired, and the truant soon disqualify themselves. Assurance, split-second decision-making, superior game skills, endurance, and the intensive practice that leads to these abilities distinguish the player from the one who "plays at" these games. Prerequisite to high achievement is a state of fitness in which cardio-respiratory endurance and strength of specific muscle groups are foremost. There are also things that an individual can do to improve her performance and specific ways that skills can be practiced.

Improving Fitness

Cardio-respiratory endurance, in very simple terms, expresses the limit to which one can go in activities that speed up the heart rate; that is, how far the individual can go before she must stop because she is "out of breath." Obviously, continually running up and down a 100-yard field tests the ability of the heart and lungs to meet the body's needs under stress.

Strength of specific muscle groups, those most used in performing soccer techniques is equally as important as endurance. Strength is an integral component of skill, for powerful kicks, long throws, fast sprints, or high jumps depend upon musculature that can exert considerable force. Good strength is also safety insurance, for a joint well protected by strong musculature is less subject to injury under the stresses of sudden starts, stops, changes of direction, and application of force. Strength does not imply "bulging" muscles. The configuration of an individual's musculature is determined primarily by the body build with which one is genetically endowed. Except in the case of the very highly trained and specialized athlete or physical worker (a state highly unlikely to be attained by girls participating in soccer or speedball), disproportionate development of muscle groups simply does not occur.

Cardio-respiratory endurance is best developed by placing slowly but steadily increasing demands upon the heart and lungs. Running is one of the best ways to build endurance, but the distance covered must be gradually lengthened or the rate stepped up for improvement to occur. Strength, flexibility, and speed are developed according to the same underlying principle as endurance: that is, the demands must be greater and greater if there is to be a positive improvement in capacity. Conditioning exercises can be a useful adjunct to game practice in attaining needed strength and agility aspects of fitness.

Fitness in the sense discussed here can be thought of as the foundation that makes possible real mastery of the techniques peculiar to soccer and speedball. Specific practice of each style of kicking, blocking, trapping, tackling, throwing, and conversion is also required, however, if the proper coordinations, movement sequences, and timing are to become automatic so as to free the player to concentrate on tactics and strategy.

Improving Performance

Responsibility for the student's progress in soccer or speedball is shared by the instructor and the student. These are not sports which individuals have much opportunity to pick up on their own. Rather, learning usually occurs in a class setting where the teacher guides the group in experiences that lead to improved performance. Nevertheless, a student who has initiative and self-motivation can easily speed up her own progress.

1. *Set specific goals that are a little beyond your present ability.* You might, for example, aim toward running three laps around the field without stopping, or kicking ten successive goals from the penalty kick mark, five to the left of center and then five to the right.
2. *Think through the basics of skills you want to develop,* as described in chapter 2. If your concern is an element of fitness, consider how to apply the overload principle. Gradually increase the demand beyond the accustomed level. Increase the rate of performance, the load, the number of repetitions, or a combination of these factors.
3. *Make a practice time schedule.* If you can arrive early to class or stay late, even a few extra minutes of practice will eventually lead to significant improvement. A free half hour now and then, particularly with several teammates, can be very profitable.
4. *Warm up* for at least five minutes before strenuous effort.

Practicing Skills

The following drills are representative of an endless variety of situations that can be set up to afford practice of techniques. Drills can be done informally without the guidance of an instructor or they may be organized for class use with instruction and coaching incorporated. Players should use free practice time to work on the techniques they perform less well and on the techniques emphasized in their own team positions. Most drills can be easily modified to include more participants, and original drills can be planned without difficulty. Usually drills should be tried first without interference by opponents. When the basic maneuver is accomplished with ease, other teammates and opponents may take their normal places on the field so that the drills become, in essence, realistic segments of the game.

It is generally agreed that the more gamelike the practice, the better the carryover into team play, and when several persons are available to work together, very realistic practices can be set up. In most cases, a competitive or self-testing element can be added to the practice also. Timing the actions performed, scoring the number of successful tries, or competing with opponents for possession of the ball help to make drills gamelike and provide a standard by which improvement can be measured. Drill 3 below, for one player, for example, affords self-competition if the number of kicks to the wall within one minute is tallied, or if a record is kept of the number of plays without a miss.

One-Player Practices

1. Dribble along the goal line, describing a circle to the left around the first goal post and then a circle to the right around the second. Reverse your direction at the corner of the field. Keep the circles small and increase the speed of the dribble (fig. 29).

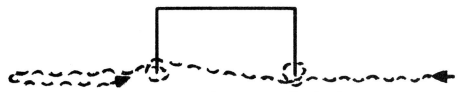

Figure 29—One Player Practice Number 1

2. Place kick the ball forward gently. Sprint to pass the ball so that you can turn to face it and trap it before it stops. Gradually increase the force of your kicks so that the sprint must be faster and farther.
3. Place kick the ball against a wall, returning the rebounds to the wall as rapidly as possible. Also try trapping the rebounds; and, for speed-ball, try converting the trapped balls to aerial balls.
4. Mark four vertical lines on a wall to represent the goal divided into thirds. Practice place kicks and shots taken on the run from different distances and angles, always aiming for one of the outer thirds of the target.

Two-Player Practices

1. Partners move down the field about seven yards apart, passing diagonally and controlling the ball with the specific techniques they have chosen to practice: inside or outside of the foot passes, instep kicks; lofted or ground balls; inside of the foot trap; lower leg trap, etc.
2. In the same formation as in no. 1, one partner dribbles forward, then makes a square pass to her partner, who plays the ball in the same manner. The pattern is continued as the players advance. By reversing direction when they reach the end of the field, the players can practice receiving and kicking from the opposite side (fig. 30).

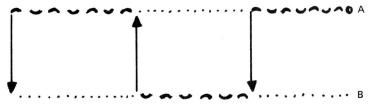

Figure 30—Two Player Practice Number 2

3. Four to six obstacles (balls, pinnies, jackets, for example are laid on the ground in a row several yards apart. A dribbles diagonally to the right and then passes behind the first obstacle to B who has circled in to receive the ball. B then dribbles diagonally to the left and passes behind the second obstacle. The pattern is continued past the last obstacle (fig. 31).

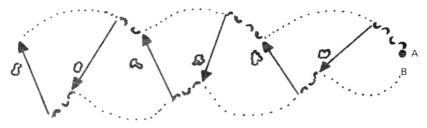

Figure 31—Two Player Practice Number 3

4. Player A drop kicks the ball from the penalty kick mark over the crossbar to her partner who is stationed behind the goal. Player B fields the ball, dribbles it to an imaginary penalty kick mark behind the goal, picks up the ball (soccer) or converts it (speedball) and drop kicks back to player A.
5. Player A punts to B who must punt back from the spot where A's punt hit the ground. Try to force the other player farther and farther back.

Three- or More Player Practices

1. *Kick-off* (all players move forward on the kick). The center forward passes diagonally to the right inner who passes to the left wing. The wing dribbles a few yards, then passes back to the center forward who traps the ball. At the end of the field, players turn around and reverse the action so that the first pass is to the left.
2. *Kick-off*. The center forward passes diagonally to the right inner who dribbles once or twice and then passes back to the center half. The center half returns the ball to the center forward who traps it. The players turn around at the end of the field and reverse the action.
3. *Kick-off* (for speedball only). Practices nos. 1 and 2 with the center forward lifting the ball to the inner so that the following passes are made with throws.
4. *Corner Kick* (soccer). Player A defends the goal; player B takes the corner kick, trying to loft the ball so that it strikes the ground in front of the goal where player C is stationed to receive and shoot by heading, blocking, or kicking. If the goalkeeper misses the ball, she retrieves it and punts back to the corner. If the ball is cleared successfully, player C retrieves and returns the ball to the corner with a place kick. When more than three players are available, they assume other positions on the attacking or defending team and the assault on the goal is continued until a score is made or the ball is cleared from the penalty area.

5. *Throw-in.* Player A, as a side halfback, positions herself to take a throw-in. Player B, as wing, moves down the field to receive the throw-in on the run. Player C, as inner, also moves forward, timing her run to get into a position diagonally ahead of the wing to receive a pass from her. The wing and inner continue to advance the ball by exchanging diagonal passes. Player A enters the field immediately after the throw-in and backs up B and C as they progress, taking control of the ball if it is overrun by A or B and returning it to them. The throw-in play is then repeated in reverse direction. The play may easily be expanded to incorporate more attacking team members or players who offer interference as defense players.

6. *Throw-in.* Players A, B, and C stand facing each other in triangular formation. A throws the ball to land at the feet of player B, who traps and passes with a side-of-the-foot pass to C. C picks up the ball and starts the drill again by executing a throw-in to A. Because the practice pattern ends before a full cycle of the three participants, the throw-in rotates on each round.

7. *Free Kick or Free Throw.* Three players, as two forwards and a halfback, stand in triangular formation. The halfback starts by taking a free kick (or, if desired, a free throw in speedball) to one of the other players. The play continues with passes from one to another, in an order preplanned for six passes. As soon as the pattern is familiar, the players move down the field, advancing the ball in the set pattern. The play ends with a touchdown pass. Other players may fill in as forwards or halfbacks. If the passing pattern after the free kick does not include each player, players should exchange positions at intervals.

6 Origin and Development of the Games

Soccer

As for many games and sports, the true origin of soccer is lost in antiquity. Numerous records show that football-type games were played in China in the second century, and it is known that games in which a ball was kicked were pastimes in Greece and Sparta. Such evidence as has been found indicates that most of these games included throwing and catching skills, which makes a more convincing case for speedball ancestry than for soccer, although rudimentary soccer elements were surely incorporated. One Greek and Spartan game was called "Harpaston." Adopted by the Romans, the title became "Harpastrum," meaning to hurl forward. When England was invaded by the Romans, the soldiers may have brought the game to Britain, where the Anglicized name "futballe" appeared. Some authorities, however, believe that a soccer-type game was played in Ireland a thousand years before the Romans set foot on English soil.

Whatever its lineage, futballe became so popular that it threatened the practice of archery during the Middle Ages. Because archery was the chief means of national defense, proficiency was essential and practice by the people was compulsory. King Edward II, therefore, tried in 1314 to stamp out the danger to England's security by issuing an edict prohibiting futballe. Apart from diverting British subjects from more serious business with bow and arrow, futballe was such a rowdy, undisciplined activity in those days that it rightly drew the disapproval of the upper classes. Poorly organized or controlled and with few rules, the games were often mob occurences leading to personal and property damage and even to loss of life. As if these handicaps were not sufficient, the Puritan influence became another factor in the attempts to suppress the sport. It is not surprising, then, that a succession of monarchs—Edward III, Richard II, Henry IV, Henry VIII, and Queen Elizabeth I—continued Edward II's ban.

The temptation to play futballe must have been overwhelming, though, because despite royal edicts, religious disapproval, and the listing of disobedience as a penal offense, the sport survived and developed. By 1603 when James I took the throne of England, firearms had negated the necessity of archery practice, and soon the King lifted the ban on futballe. By 1863 organized rules had been drawn up by the Football Association of London for the sport, by then called "Association Football."

As early as 1820, soccer games were played in the United States between Harvard and Yale as part of the freshman hazing process. Once again, unfortunately, the sport caused so many injuries that another ban was imposed, this time by the colleges concerned. And once again, soccer proved too hardy to kill. Princeton and Rutgers revived school and college play by making arrangements in 1868 for an intercollegiate match the following year.

Until 1900, when soccer was first included in the Olympic Games, the sport was governed by diverse sets of rules. The need for unification was undoubtedly pointed up by the Olympic competition, and in 1904 an organization to meet this problem was formed. Now the same regulations apply from country to country.

The most important tournament to soccer players and fans is the competition begun in 1930 for the Jules Remet trophy, better known as the "World Cup." Entries are received from most of the nations of the world, and the games are scheduled every four years midway between Olympic games. In 1970, Brazil retired the Cup by defeating Italy and thereby winning its third victory in the tournament. World championships will continue to be determined, although Brazil now has permanent possession of the Jules Remet trophy.

Speedball

Most games and sports gradually evolved over centuries of play, but speedball was originated in response to a specific need—the need for a new fall season intramural sport for men at the University of Michigan. What was desired was a simple, adaptable game, inexpensive to play and easy to administer, involving play with the hands, and with techniques and rules based on already familiar activities. The inspiration for the basic design of the game came to Elmer D. Mitchell, then Director of Intramurals at the University, as he was watching a baseball game. A fielder attempting to catch a fly ball deflected it to a teammate. Since the ball had not touched the ground, it remained in play until the teammate held it securely; then the "out" was called. This play sparked the idea of a sport combining one set of rules for aerial play and another for ground play.

Various means of scoring were considered and tried. Techniques and regulations were borrowed from soccer, basketball, and Australian rugby (a form of football). A few unique skills were devised for converting a ground ball to an aerial ball. One technique, the aerial dribble, was even introduced by chance when a good basketball player juggled the ball as he received it and met an opponent simultaneously.

The new sport was tried out in intramural play in the fall of 1921. During the game, one of the players called out to his teammates, "Let's speed the ball." The quality of speed being the very essence of the sport, "speedball" was acclaimed as a fitting title.

Dr. Mitchell's invention was introduced to the rest of the United States in an article written by George Pierrot which appeared in the then widely-read magazine, *The American Boy*. Speedball enjoyed an immediate and enthusiastic response. California promoted the sport through its State Di-

Can you set up a scoring system so that you can test your ability to perform One Player Practices 3 and 4? Two Player Practice 4?

rector of Physical Education, and other states followed suit. Girls and women began to participate under men's rules in about 1923 and in that same year the Tennessee Coal, Iron and Railway Company included speedball in its industrial league play. In 1930, the National Section on Women's Athletics (later known as the Division for Girls and Women's Sports) appointed a Speedball Committee to revise the men's rules to make them more suitable for women's play.

Today the men's and women's games remain similar in fundamental respects but surprisingly different in rules, yet the character of the play does not seem to be materially affected. Terminology, field dimensions, and the scoring system are three of the several points of divergence.

Language of the Games

7

Terms and Definitions
Common to Soccer and Speedball

Attacking Team—Team in possession of the ball.

Backing Up—Player moving in behind teammate to assist with the play if needed.

Centering—Moving ball from near the sideline toward center of the field, particularly in preparation for a field goal try.

Clearing—Sending ball away from vicinity of goal.

Covering—Occupying a space in order to block an opening for pass or maneuver by opponent.

Defending Team—Team not in possession of ball; also sometimes refers to team whose goal is threatened.

Double Foul—Rules violation committed simultaneously by a member of each team.

Dribbling—Succession of kicks by means of which player advances ball under control.

Drop Kick—Technique in which ball is dropped to the ground and kicked just as it rebounds.

Feint—Deceptive movement to mislead an opponent as to player's intention.

Goal Mouth—Opening bounded by goal posts and crossbar.

Half-volley—Kick in which ball is contacted just as it rebounds after falling to ground.

Handling—Foul called for playing ball illegally by touching it with hand or arm when they are not in total contact with the body.

Heading—Playing ball by meeting it with the head.

Holding—Foul called for impeding progress of an opponent by touching her with hand or extended arm.

Kick-off—Place kick taken at center of halfway line to start play in each quarter and after scoring each goal. Teams are in their own ends of field for kick-off, with defending team behind their restraining line.

Lead Pass—Pass directed ahead of receiver so she can gain control of ball without reducing her speed.

Lobbing or Lofting—Kicking ball so that it rises from the ground.

Marking—Following a player's moves with intention of preventing her from receiving ball or playing it effectively.

Own Goal—Goal a team is defending.

Own Half of Field—Half in which team's own goal is located.

Pass Back—Pass sent in backward direction, usually from fullback under pressure to the goalkeeper.

Place Kick—Kick taken while ball is stationary on ground.

Punt—Kick in which ball is dropped and contacted before it strikes the ground.

Save—Preventing ball from entering goal.

Trapping—Stopping progress of ball by securing it with foot or feet or between leg or legs and the ground.

Volley—Contacting ball while it is in the air and directing it toward a teammate.

Terms and Definitions
Specific to Soccer

Carrying—Rules infringement by goalkeeper committed by taking more than two steps while holding ball.

Corner Kick—Place kick awarded to attacking team after ball has been sent over crossbar or over goal line outside the goal posts by team guarding the goal. Taken on goal line 5 yards from nearest corner. Teammates of kicker and defending forwards are in field of play; defending backfield is behind goal line.

Defense Kick—Place kick awarded to defending team after ball has been sent over crossbar or over goal line outside goal posts by attacking team. Kick may be taken anywhere on quarter circles bounding penalty area.

Direct Free Kick—Free kick from which goal may be scored directly. Taken on spot where foul occurred.

Foul—Any of following illegal acts: tripping, kicking, striking, holding, pushing, or jumping at opponent; unnecessary roughness; handling ball except by goalkeeper; failure to notify umpire when goalkeeper is changed and new goalkeeper handles ball in penalty area; or illegal substitution. (See also *Infringement*.)

Infringement—Any of following illegal acts: improperly taking free kick, corner kick, kick-off, penalty kick, defense kick, or roll-in; being offside; or improperly using goalkeeper's privileges.

Indirect Free Kick—Free kick from which goal may not be scored directly. Kick is taken on spot where infringement occurred.

Offside—Infringement referring to illegal position of a player when *all three* of these conditions obtain: (1) player is in opponent's half of field; (2) there are fewer than three opponents nearer to their goal line than the player; and (3) player is ahead of ball at moment it is played by one of her own team.

Penalty Kick—Place kick taken 12 yards in front of goal by attacking team. Usually awarded for foul committed by defending team within penalty area.

Roll-in—Method of putting ball in play to give equal advantage to both teams. Two opponents stand 5 yards apart, each facing opponents' goal. Umpire stands 5 yards from opponents and rolls ball between them.

Throw-In—Means of putting ball in play after it has been sent wholly over side line by one team. A member of opposite team stands outside field of play opposite point where ball crosses line and throws ball back into field in any direction.

Terms and Definitions
Specific to Speedball

Aerial Ball—One that has been raised into air directly from a kick or one that has not yet touched ground after a throw.

Air Dribble—Technique in which player throws or taps ball and then touches it again before it reaches the ground or is touched by another player.

Blocking—Intercepting ball with any part of body. Hands and arms need not be in contact with body to block aerial balls. Also designates foul called for impeding progress of opponent with or without the ball by means of body contact.

Charging—Foul called for moving one's body or ball against an opponent whose path or position has been established.

Foul—See Individual Foul and Team Foul.

Ground Ball—One that has touched the ground since it was last kicked or thrown. A ground ball may be stationary, rolling, or bouncing.

Holding The Ball—Foul called for retaining ball in hands more than 5 seconds out-of-bounds or for a free kick; taking more than 10 seconds for penalty kick.

Individual Foul—Any of following illegal acts: blocking, charging, pushing, tagging, hacking, holding, tripping; handling ground ball, traveling, holding the ball; unnecessary roughness, threatening eyes of player holding the ball; delaying game; air dribbling more than once, or trying a drop kick for goal or touchdown pass while within penalty area.

Kick-up—Technique for converting ground ball to aerial ball. Player may kick-up by letting ball roll up her foot or leg provided ball is in air before it is caught, or she may lift ball with one or two feet.

Penalty Kick—Drop kick taken 12 yards in front of goal by attacking team. Usually awarded for foul committed by defending team within penalty area.

Tagging—Foul called for repeatedly touching opponent with hand, elbow, or body.

Team Foul—Any of following illegal acts: taking more than three time-outs in a game; illegal substitution; or having more than eleven players of one team on the field.

Throw-In—Means of putting ball in play after it has been sent wholly over any boundary line by one team. A member of other team stands outside field of play opposite point where ball crossed line and throws ball back into field in any direction.

Traveling With The Ball—Foul called for taking more than one step after receiving ball while stationary or taking more than two steps after receiving ball while running.

8

Rules of the Games

The official rules are published by the Division for Girls and Women's Sports of the American Association for Health, Physical Education and Recreation and may be purchased from the Association headquarters located at 1201 16th St., N. W., Washington, D. C., 20036. A digest of the most important rules specific to each of the two games follows. (Definitions of the terms may be found in chapter 7, pages 51-53).

Soccer and speedball are played on a rectangular field by two teams of eleven members each: five forwards, three halfbacks, two fullbacks, and a goalkeeper. The object of the play is to score more points than the opponents by advancing the ball down the field and sending it across the opponents' goal line by means that are specific to each sport, while preventing the opponents from doing the same. In both games playing time is divided into 4 quarters, each 8 minutes in length, with a 2-minute rest interval after the first and third quarters and a 10-minute rest interval between halves. A defaulted game is scored as 2-0, and the score of a tie game stands. Officiating is performed by two umpires, two scorekeepers, and two timekeepers (figs. 32 and 33).

The team winning the toss has the option of either choosing which goal it will defend during the first half of the game or of deciding which team shall start the game by taking the first kick-off. The team kicking off may not cross the halfway line, the opponents may not cross the restraining line, and no player may be closer than 5 yards until the ball has been kicked. After a goal the team scored against kicks off. Teams alternate kicking off at the start of each quarter.

Rules Specific to Soccer

Playing Privileges

The ball may be kicked, dribbled, blocked, volleyed, headed, or trapped by any player. The goalkeeper within her penalty area is uniquely privileged to pick up the ball and hold it up to 3 seconds, bounce it once, throw it, drop kick or punt it, combine the bounce with a throw or kick, or substitute two steps for the bounce.

Scoring

Two points are scored for a field goal by kicking, volleying, or heading the ball between the goal posts and under the cross bar. One point is given

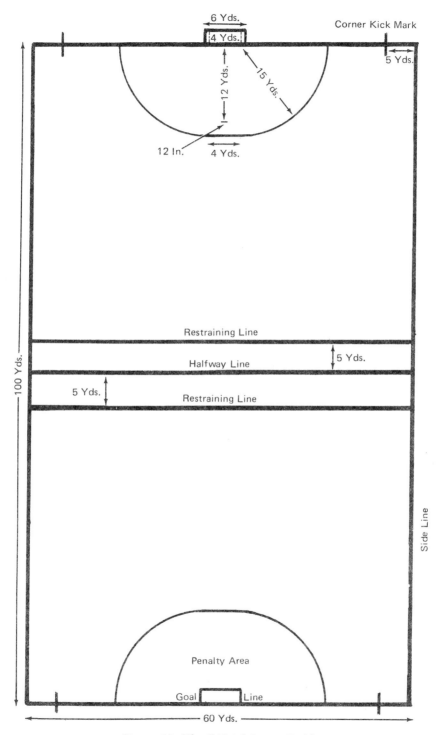

Figure 32—The Official Soccer Field

55

for a successful penalty kick. A goal may be made from anywhere on the field and from a direct free kick, a roll-in, or a corner kick. A goal may not be made directly from a kick-off, a defense kick, or an indirect free kick.

Interruption of Play

The Ball is Out of Bounds When	The Ball is Put Back Into Play By
It goes out of bounds:	
1. Through the goal in legal manner.	Kick-off by team scored against.
2. Over the sideline.	Throw-in by opposing team at point where ball left the field.
3. Over the sideline off two opponents.	Roll-in between the two opponents 5 yards in from point where ball left the field.
4. Over the goal line by attackers.	Defense kick by defending team.
5. Over the goal line by defenders.	Corner kick by attacking team.
A rules infringement occurs.	Indirect free kick by opposing team at spot where infringement occurred.
A foul is committed by either team outside the penalty area, by the attacking team inside the penalty area, or by actions that result in disqualification of a player(s).	Direct free kick by opposing team at spot where foul occurred.
A foul is committed by the defending team within the penalty area.	Penalty kick by opposing team.
An infringement or foul is committed simultaneously by both teams.	Roll-in where act occurred (taken at least 5 yards in from goal or boundary line).
The umpire signals "time-out."	The play that would normally occur next or, if there is none, where play was suspended.

Regulations Governing Soccer Plays

Play	Regulations	Penalty if any of the Regulations is Not Met
Kick-off	Team taking kick-off may not cross center line and defenders may not cross restraining line until ball is kicked; ball must travel forward at least distance of circumference; no player closer than 5 yards; kicker may not play ball again until it is played by another person.	Indirect free kick for opposing team.
Throw-in	Thrower must stand outside field of play on spot; thrower may not play ball again until it is played by another person; no player closer than 5 yards.	Throw-in for opposing team.

Play	Regulations	Penalty if any of the Regulations is Not Met
Defense Kick	Ball must travel forward at least distance of its circumference; kicker may not play ball again until it is played by another person; teammates must be at least 5 yards away. Opponents must be at least 5 yards away.	Indirect free kick for opposing team. Repeat defense kick.
Corner Kick	Defending backfield behind goal line; defending team at least 5 yards away. Ball must travel at least distance of its circumference; kicker may not play ball again until it is played by another person.	Repeat corner kick. Indirect free kick for opposing team.
Roll-in	All players must be at least 5 yards away.	Indirect free kick for opposing team.
Free Kick	Ball must travel at least distance of circumference; kicker may not play ball again until it is played by another person; teammates must be at least 5 yards away. Defending team must be at least 5 yards away.	Indirect free kick for opposing team. Repeat free kick.
Penalty Kick	Ball must travel forward at least distance of its circumference; attacking team must be in field of play until ball is kicked. Defending team must be in field of play until ball is kicked (goalkeeper on goal line).	Indirect free kick for opposing team. Repeat penalty kick.

Rules Specific to Speedball

Situations not covered are governed by the official soccer or basketball rules.

Playing Privileges

In addition to the soccer methods of playing the ball, all players may catch, throw, tap, air dribble once, punt, or drop kick an "aerial" ball. An aerial ball may be played with the feet or body if desired, and may be tapped or taken from an opponent. A player may legally guard an opponent.

Scoring

Points are earned in four ways. A field goal (2 points) is scored by volleying or heading a ground ball between the goal posts under the crossbar. A drop kick from the field of play may be used to score a field goal, but a punt may not. Three points are scored for a drop kick from the field

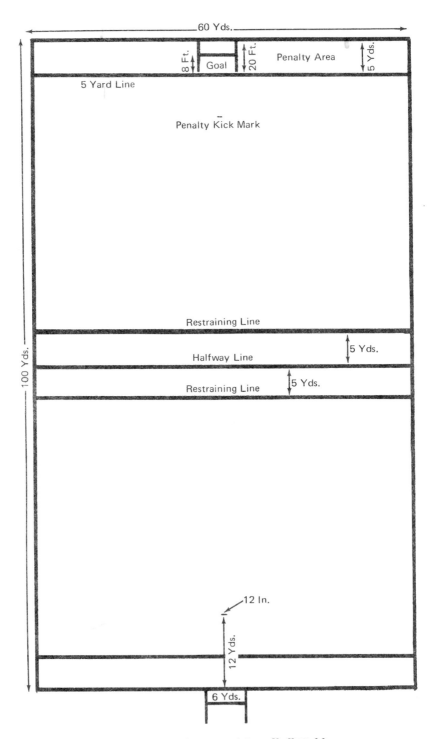

Figure 33–The Official Speedball Field

of play which goes over the crossbar and between the goal posts. One point is given for a penalty kick, which is made by a drop kick over the crossbar from the penalty kick mark. Two points are awarded for a touchdown, which is a throw from the field of play caught by a teammate behind the opponents' goal line but not between the goal posts. A field goal may be scored directly from a kick-off or a free kick. A touchdown may be scored directly from a free throw from the field of play.

Interruption of Play

The Ball is Out of Play When	The Ball is Put Back Into Play By
It goes out of bounds:	
1. As a goal is scored.	Kick-off by team scored against.
2. Over the sideline.	Throw-in by opposing team at point where ball left field.
3. Over the sideline or goal line off two opponents.	Toss-up between the two opponents 5 yards in from point where ball left field.
4. Over the goal line without scoring.	Kick-in by opposing team at point where ball left field.
An individual foul occurs:	
1. By a player outside her own penalty area.	Free kick by opposing team for a ground ball foul or an unguarded throw for an aerial ball foul at spot where foul occurred.
2. By a player within her own penalty or behind her own goal line.	Penalty kick by opposing team.
3. By the attacking team behind the opponents' goal line.	Free kick or throw by the opposing team on the goal line opposite where foul occurred.
A team foul occurs.	Penalty kick by opposing team.
A double foul occurs.	Toss-up between the two offenders where foul occurred (taken at least 5 yards in from boundary line).
The umpire signals "time-out."	The play that would normally occur next or, if there is none, by a toss-up where play was suspended.

Regulations Governing Speedball Plays

Play	Regulations	If Regulation is Violated
Kick-off	Same as soccer (see p. 57).	Same as soccer except substitute free kick.
Throw-in	Same as soccer (see p. 57).	Same as soccer.
Free Kick	Same as soccer (see p. 58).	Same as soccer except substitute free kick for indirect free kick.

In speedball, may a touchdown be scored directly from a free throw, from a pass from within the penalty area, from a pass caught behind the goal line and between the goal posts?

Play	Regulations	If Regulation is Violated
Free Throw	Ball must travel at least distance of circumference; thrower may not play ball again until it is played by another person; all players must be at least 5 yards away.	Free kick by opposing team.
Penalty Kick	Ball must be dropkicked so that it bounces behind penalty kick mark prior to kick; attacking team must be in field of play and at least 5 yards away; kicker may not play ball again until it has been played by another person. All defenders must be behind goal line or in field of play and at least 5 yards away until ball is kicked (only the goalkeeper may be behind goal mouth).	Free kick by opposing team. Repeat penalty kick.
Toss-up	No player closer than 5 yards. Player may not tap ball before it reaches highest point; tap it more than twice; catch ball; play it again before it touches ground.	Free kick by opposing team.

Selected References

A.A.H.P.E.R., *Soccer-Speedball, Flag Football Guide.* Washington, D. C., 20036. Published every two years. Official rules, information about officiating and competition, articles about various aspects of the sports.

Barnes, Mildred J. *How to Improve Your Soccer, for Girls.* Chicago: Recreational Films, Inc., 1967. Fundamental skills and team tactics presented photographically.

Csanadi, Arpad. *Soccer,* vol. 2, *Training.* New York: Corvina Press (Sportshelf) 1965. An exceedingly comprehensive and detailed analysis of the men's game. Recommended for dedicated enthusiasts and instructors.

Fait, Hollis (ed.), *Speedball for Men.* Washington, D. C.: A.A.H.P.E.R., 1201 16th St., N.W., Washington, D. C., 20036, 1967. Individual chapters by different authors on speedball history, techniques, rules adaptations, evaluation, and other topics.

Meyer, Margaret H. and Schwarz, Marguerite M. *Team Sports for Girls and Women.* 4th ed. Philadelphia: W. B. Saunders, 1965. The most comprehensive treatment of the women's game, much of the information in outline form. Recommended for instructors and serious students of the sports.

Miller, Donna Mae and Ley, Katherine. *Individual and Team Sports for Women.* New York: Prentice-Hall, Inc., 1955. Information on all aspects of soccer and speedball including teaching and lead-up games.

Schmid, Irwin R., Schmid, Melvin, and McKeon, John. *Skills and Strategies of Successful Soccer.* Englewood Cliffs, New Jersey: Prentice-Hall, Inc., 1968. Thorough coverage of complexities of men's game as well as basic techniques.

Sevy, Ruth (ed.). *Selected Soccer and Speedball Articles.* Washington, D. C.:
A.A.H.P.E.R., 1963. Articles on practice games, techniques, drills, officiating,
and evaluation of skill.

Articles

Dameron, Mary Jane. "Fitness for Soccer." D.G.W.S. *Soccer-Speedball Guide,*
1966-68, pp. 49-50. Activities that develop endurance.

Maule, Tex. "Pelé and Pals Retire the Cup," *Sports Illustrated,* 26 (June 29, 1970),
pp. 24-25.

Maule, Tex. "Soccer Is a Frenzy," *Sports Illustrated,* 25 (June 22, 1970), pp. 12-17.

Michener, James A. "Soccer's Wild World Cup Scramble," *Reader's Digest,* 96,
no. 578 (June, 1970), pp. 173-74; 179-82.

Miguel, Acoca. "Mighty Spectacle of Soccer," *Life,* 61 (August 26, 1966), pp.
81-89.

Shimek, Anne. "Soccer Visual Aids," D.G.W.S. *Soccer-Speedball Guide,* 1968-
1970, pp. 47-48. List of films, filmstrips, and teaching aids including distributor's addresses.

Thorpe, Jo Anne. "Self Testing in Soccer Skills," D.G.W.S. *Soccer-Speedball
Guide,* 1966-1968, pp. 25-30. Activities for evaluating soccer skills.

Audio-visual Materials

Soccer-Girls, 1969. Distributor: Athletic Institute, 805 Merchandise Mart, Chicago, Illinois 60654. Color filmstrip; 6 units, si. with guide, $40.50; 6 units,
sd. with records, materials, 600 Madison Ave., New York, N. Y., 10022. Strips
cover background information about the game, techniques, and tactics.

Index